STUDYING ROM

Classical World Series

Classical World Series

STUDYING ROMAN LAW

Paul J. du Plessis

Bristol Classical Press

First published in 2012 by
Bristol Classical Press
an imprint of
Bloomsbury Academic
Bloomsbury Publishing Plc
50 Bedford Square
London WC1B 3DP, UK

CIP records for this book are available from the
British Library and the Library of Congress

ISBN 978-1780930268

Typeset by Ray Davies
Printed and bound in Great Britain by
the MPG Books Group

www.bloomsburyacademic.com

Contents

Date/Emperor	Historical events	Legally significant developments	Juristic developments
Julio-Claudian Dynasty			
27 BCE–14 CE Augustus	27 BCE Octavian is granted the title of Augustus by the senate. Effective end of the Roman Republic		Statutory abolition of the *Legis Actio* procedure Creation of the *ius respondendi*
	15 BCE Campaign in the upper Danube region	18-17 BCE. *Lex Iulia de Maritandis Ordinibus*; *Lex Iulia de Adulteriis Coercendis*; *Leges Iulia iudiciorum privatorum et publicorum*	Jurists of the period include Capito, Labeo, Fabius Mela
		2 BCE *Lex Fufia Caninia*	
	2 CE Exile of Julia	4 CE *Lex Aelia Sentia*	Jurists of the period include Nerva (pater) and Massurius Sabinus
	9 CE Battle of the Teutoburg Forest: Rhine becomes the Western boundary of the Roman Empire	9 CE *Lex Papia Poppaea*	
14-37 CE Tiberius	14 CE Disturbances in Rhine and Danube areas	19 CE *Lex Iunia Norbana*	
	32 CE Grain shortages, protests in Rome	28 CE *Lex Iunia Velleia*	
	34 CE Province of Syria enlarged		
37-41 CE Caligula			*Ius respondendi* likely awarded to the heads of the two law schools
41-54 CE Claudius	43 CE Lycia becomes a Province		

Emperors	Events	Legislation	Jurists
54-68 CE Nero	43 CE First invasion of Britain 46 CE Thrace becomes a province 51 CE Grain shortages, protests in Rome 61 CE Revolt of Boudicca 64 CE Great fire in Rome; state prosecutions of Christians commence 65 CE Conspiracy to assassinate Nero	*c.* 46 CE *Senatusconsultum Velleianum* 52 CE *Senatusconsultum Claudianum*	Jurists of the period include Nerva (filius), Longinus and Proculus
68-69 CE <u>Year of the four Emperors</u> Galba, Otho, Vitellius, Vespasian			
<u>Flavian Dynasty</u> 69-79 CE Vespasian	70 CE Destruction of Jerusalem 70 CE Judea becomes a Roman province 77 CE Roman conquest of Britian resumes	*Senatusconsultum Macedonianum* (uncertain date) *Lex de imperio Vespasiani*	Jurists of the period include Caecilius Sabinus
79-81 CE Titus 81-96 CE Domitian	79 CE Eruption of Vesuvius 80 CE Flavian Amphitheatre opened 83 CE Battle of Mons Graupius in Scotland; Britain (England and Wales) becomes a Roman province 84 CE Disturbances on Rhine frontier 93 CE Stoics expelled from Rome		Jurists of the period include Pegasus

Date/Emperor	Historical events	Legally significant developments	Juristic developments
Nerva-Antonine Dynasty			
96-98 CE Nerva			
97-117 CE Trajan	101-102 CE First Dacian War 105-106 CE Second Dacian War 106 CE Dacia becomes a province 106 CE Arabia becomes a Roman province 111 CE Pliny sent as governor to Bythinia 112 CE Trajan's Column erected 114 CE Armenia becomes a province 115 CE Mesopotamia becomes a province	97 CE *Lex Agraria* (final piece of legislation to be enacted by the popular assemblies)	Jurists of the period include Iavolenus Priscus, Titius Aristo, Celsus (filius), Neratius Priscus, Octavenus, Salvius Iulianus Effective end of the *ius respondendi*.
117-138 CE Hadrian	117 CE Empire-wide revolts 126 CE Hadrian's Wall completed 131 CE Bar-Kokhba Revolt 131-135 CE Jewish uprising in Palestine suppressed (Jews prevented from entering Jerusalem)	130 CE *Senatusconsultum Tertulliaum* 135 CE *Edictum Perpetuum*	
138-161 CE Antoninus Pius	142 CE Antonine Wall completed; Devaluation of the currency		

Emperors / Dynasty	Events	Laws	Jurists
161-169 CE Lucius Verus	167 CE Major Germanic invasion of the Empire thwarted	*Senatusconsultum Orfitianum*	Jurists of the period include Pomponius; Institutes of Gaius written
161-180 CE Marcus Aurelius (reigned from 161 as co-regent with Lucius Verus until his death)			Jurists of the period include S. Caecilius Africanus; Maecianus, Terentius Clemens, Saturninus, Florentinus; Ulpius Marcellus
177-192 CE Commodus	Fiscal problems across the Empire		
193 CE <u>Year of the five Emperors</u> Pertinax, Didius Julianus, Pescennius Niger, Septimius Severus			
<u>Severan Dynasty</u> 193-211 CE Septimius Severus			
198-217 CE Caracalla	212 CE *Constitutio Antoniniana*		
217-218 CE Macrinus and Diadumedianus			

Date/Emperor	Historical events	Legally significant developments	Juristic developments
218-222 CE Eliogabalus			Jurists of the period include Papinianus, Tryphoninus, Ulpianus, Paulus
222-235 CE Alexander Severus			Modestinus, the last 'named' Roman jurist of the classical period
The crisis of the third century	238 CE Revolts in North Africa		
	260 CE Many of the Empire's frontiers under attack		
284-305 CE Diocletian			

This timeline is based on information from the following sources: P.J. Du Plessis, *Borkowski's Textbook on Roman Law* 3rd edn (Oxford 2009) – Timeline (online resources); C.E. Robinson, *A History of the Roman Republic* 2nd edn (London 1937), 455-66; M. Carey and H.H. Scullard, *A History of Rome* 3rd edn (London 1992), 559-70; O.E. Tellegen-Couperus, *A Short History of Roman Law* (London/New York 1993), 150-65 as well as *Cassell's Chronology of World History* (London 2005). Information about legislation is based on the chronology in J.E. Spruit, *Enchridium: Een Geschiedenis van het Romeinse Privaatrecht* 4th edn (Deventer 1994) 306-13.

Preface

This book was written chiefly as a brief guide for those wishing to obtain a basic overview of the state of Roman private law during the first three centuries of the Common Era. It should not be treated as a substitute for a technical manual on Roman law and it was not written for that purpose. As a work of an introductory nature, it does not contain a detailed account of all of the intricacies and technicalities of Roman legal rules as there are many excellent recent works on the subject. Rather, this book is aimed at a non-specialist audience wishing to gain a basic introduction to the subject before progressing to more specialist works.

This book focuses solely on Roman private law, the body of legal rules which operate between individuals, as this is the most commonly studied area of Roman law. It must not be forgotten that a rich body of Roman public and criminal law also exists which are fields of study in their own right.

October 2011   PdP

Translations and Abbreviations

The provenance of all translations used in this work is provided in square brackets at the end of each passage. In most cases, these references are to books which may be located in the bibliography, with the exception of (a) those translations which are my own and are labelled as such and (b) those deriving from a set of Handouts used to teach Roman law at the University of Edinburgh.

BCE	Before the Common Era
C	Codex Iustinianus
CE	The Common Era
D	Digesta
FIRA	Fontes Iuris Romani Anteiustiniani
Inst.Gai.	Institutes of Gaius
P.Oxy	Oxyrynchus Papyri
TPSulp	Tabulae Pompeianae Sulpiciorum

Chapter 1

Sources and methods

It is a human trait to attempt to make sense out of seemingly random events. Nowhere is this more evident than in the study of the past which to many people seems little more than a random collection of battles, conquests and plagues. In order to make sense of these seemingly random events, much of the academic study of the past has traditionally been concerned with the identification of smaller periods. By studying these periods in great detail, historians are able to better understand the past as a whole and to identify larger 'themes' or 'trends' which characterise specific smaller periods. Roman history is a good example. Historians tend to divide the time during which the Romans dominated the Mediterranean world into three broad periods: the Monarchy (*c*. 753-510 BCE), the Republic (509-27 BCE) and the Empire (*c*. 27 BCE-476 CE). No one would deny the utility or accuracy of these labels, since they describe the dominant form of state during each period, but it must never be forgotten that such labels, even if they are useful attempts to divide the past into smaller periods of study, are by their very nature generic and mask a great level of detail. Take for example the period of the Empire. After the crisis of the third century CE, the constitutional structure of the Roman state was utterly transformed to the extent that it bore little resemblance to what had come before. Thus, although it makes sense to classify this entire period as one of 'Empire', the early Empire in many ways bears little resemblance to the later Empire. Any student of the past should therefore always be critical when confronted with accepted periodisations (see Riggsby, *Roman Law*, 20-2).

Within the broad discipline of Roman studies, historians who specialise in specific aspects of Roman civilisation such as the law often employ their own system of periodisation. Roman law is a good example. Scholars of Roman law tend to divide the three periods mentioned above into smaller segments based on the state of the law. This is a classic example of a system of classification based on a specific ideology, namely to construct a grand story about 'continuity' or 'rise and fall'. The first of these, the so-called 'archaic' period (*c*. 753-250 BCE), spans the Monarchy and the first two centuries of the Republic. The second period (250-*c*. 27 BCE), conventionally known as the 'pre-classical' period, (the middle to late Republic) is a period of great social and legal change and acts as formative era for the period to follow. The third period (*c.* 27 BCE-284 CE), known as the 'classical' period of Roman law, was the high-point of intellectual development when Roman law matured into a sophisticated body of law. While this may be true, this form of periodisation also masks a period of enormous social change (from Principate to Dominate) and includes the third century when the Roman state experienced great political upheaval. Similarly, the fourth period (*c.* 284-476 CE in the West/527 CE in the East), the 'post-classical period', is a complex time in the history of the Roman Empire. The Empire had been divided into two administrative units during the reign of Diocletian and the increasingly unstable political situation in the Western Empire undermined the rule of law. The extent to which this position differed from that in the East is difficult to ascertain and leaves one with the distinct impression that the conventional classification of this period as one of simplification and decline, summed up in the term 'post-classical period', requires some revision. The final period, commonly known as the 'Justinianic period' (527-565 CE) encompasses the reign of Justinian in the Eastern Roman Empire. The reign of this emperor is seminal to modern understanding of Roman law, owing to his endeavours to collect all of Roman law and redact it into a useful set of volumes to be used by scholars and courts alike.

This brief account of the periodisation commonly used by scholars of Roman law shows that it is driven by its own ideology. Its main aim is to demonstrate the intellectual ascendancy of Roman law during the classical period and its restoration in the Byzantine period during the reign of Justinian. The other periods are merely seen as either formative or transitory. Whether such assessments are correct is a matter for another book, but it is worth repeating that periodisations are modern preoccupations and open to revision.

This book will focus solely on the 'classical period' of Roman law. It is the period for which we have most evidence in the sources. But focusing on one period alone will not place Roman law in its broader context. To that end it is important to provide a potted history of the other periods in order to form a clearer picture of the law during the classical period.

The 'archaic' period (*c.* 753-250 BCE) covers the entire span of the Monarchy and the first two and a half centuries of the Republic. This period starts with the well-known tale of Aeneas and a group of Trojan refugees fleeing a burning Troy and ends with Rome in a battle with Carthage over trade routes in the Mediterranean. In the intervening period, Roman civilisation grew from an insignificant free city founded by the descendants of Aeneas into a formidable political presence on the Italian mainland. Much surrounding the founding of Rome by the twins Romulus and Remus is myth, but archaeological evidence shows that three powerful tribes, the Latins, Sabines and Etruscans, were present in the area surrounding the future site of the city of Rome during the eighth century BCE. It is likely that these three tribes, through conquest and intermarriage, were the true ancestors of the Romans. According to legend, Rome was ruled by seven elected kings until 510 BCE when, following a popular revolt, King Tarquin 'the haughty' was deposed. Later authors credited the kings, by virtue of their royal decrees, with the creation of many of the most revered institutions of the Roman state, such as the senate, the division of the populace into voting bodies known as *comitiae* and the patriarchal system based on paternal authority. Whether these kings (or their decrees) ever existed cannot be ascertained, but the Roman belief in them was perhaps more important.

In 509 BCE, the Roman state was reorganised into a Republic, headed by two annually elected officials known as consuls and assisted in matters of state by the senate (a body of men drawn from the most prominent aristocratic families). In time, further offices were added to deal with certain aspects of state administration. These included the praetorship (in 367 BCE), an office created (according to some) to deal with the administration of justice. A number of important societal advances occurred during the first two centuries of the Republic. A written alphabet appeared and coined money was introduced. Some territorial expansion had occurred under the Monarchy and this policy was pursued further during the early years of the Republic. The consequence was that the citizens of Rome (mainly plebeians – the lower orders of society) were conscripted to fight in these territorial wars as Rome did not yet possess a professional standing army. In a largely agrarian society, the absence of the plebeians during times of war caused popular discontent and on more than one occasion the plebeians threatened to secede. These threats, collectively known as 'the struggle of the orders', were used with great effect to secure constitutional concessions at the expense of the patricians – the aristocratic section of Roman society. One of the most prominent of these concessions was the enactment of the Twelve Tables, the first piece of legislation aimed at making the law accessible to the entire populace. Another important piece of legislation was the *Lex Hortensia* in 287 BCE, which stated that decisions of the council of the plebs would henceforth bind the populace (not just the plebeians) without requiring ratification by the senate. Throughout the fourth and the third centuries BCE, territorial expansion continued so that by the end of this period, through a series of alliances and by the granting of citizenship to newly conquered tribes, the Romans had become the dominant force in Italy.

Knowledge of the law during this period is limited. It is generally assumed that, like many agrarian societies of the ancient world, 'archaic' Roman law consisted largely of unwritten customs which contained both legal and religious norms. Royal decrees, if they existed, must have been no more than additions to existing custom. The institutions reputed to have been created during the Monarchy, such as the senate and the popular assemblies (including the council of the plebeians in 471 BCE), had an important impact on the development of Roman law during the Republic (since only the latter could enact statute). Furthermore, the establishment of fundamental notions such as the distinction between plebeian and patrician, the system of clans and the patriarchal family structure would prove to have a significant impact on the development of Roman law. It is not clear whether the change in constitutional structure from Monarchy to Republic had an immediate impact on the state of Roman private law. Much of the law appears to have remained customary. One of the most important legal changes which occurred roughly sixty years after the fall of the Monarchy was the enactment of the Twelve Tables, a compilation of more controversial areas of Roman customary law (mainly concerning the family, property and succession). Much uncertainty prevails surrounding the enactment of this law. It is said to have been modelled on a Greek law code (that of Solon), but there is little evidence in the text of the law to support this. It may well be that the story about Greek influence was an attempt during the Hellenistic period to link the origins of Roman law with Greek philosophy. The truth of this account (and the connection between the first piece of Roman legislation and Greece) cannot be verified, but the Romans of subsequent generations believed it to be so, and this is perhaps more important than the factual accuracy of the claim.

Following the constitutional transformation from elected Monarchy to Republic, Royal decrees were replaced with statutes enacted by the voting assemblies (*comitiae*). Other than the Twelve Tables, four statutes enacted during this period may be said to have had a significant impact on the development of Roman law. The first was a group of statutes collectively called the *Leges Liciniae Sextiae* of 367 BCE. These effectively ended the struggle of the orders by providing that at least one of the consuls had to be a plebeian. Since each consul had the right to veto the decisions of the other this created a constitutional balance. It also created the office of the praetor, an official charged with the administration of Rome's courts and thus with the development of the law. It was not until about 150 BCE, however, that the praetor started to influence legal development overtly. The reasons for this delay are complex and lie chiefly in the change of court procedure. Another important statute was the *Lex Poetelia* of 326 BCE which reformed the law on the private imprisonment of debtors. Under the Twelve Tables, a creditor had extensive rights of imprisonment and, in extreme cases, could even deprive the debtor of his liberty by selling him as a slave. These rights were curtailed by this act. Two further statutes deserve mention. First, the *Lex Hortensia* of 287 BCE, another victory for the plebeians, permitted the council of the plebeians to make laws, similar to the capacity enjoyed by the other *comitiae*, which bound the whole of the Roman populace without requiring the ratification of the senate. Finally, the *Lex Aquilia*, of an uncertain date, but probably after 287 BCE, reformed the law on wrongful damage to property by augmenting the existing provisions in the Twelve Tables with a new mode for calculating financial loss.

Information is scarce about courts and court procedure during the 'archaic' period. The Twelve Tables mentions a rudimentary court procedure (summons, trial and execution of the judgement) based on ritual 'actions-at-law', but does not elaborate on the composition of the court or its location. It is generally assumed that during the Monarchy (apart from family councils headed by the head of the household who presided over domestic jurisdiction by virtue of his paternal power) the king advised by the senate administered justice. Following the transition to a Republic, this function was initially taken over by the consuls until the office of praetor was created in 367 BCE. The oldest form of court procedure was based on the actions-at-law: five highly formal actions (i.e. rituals) which had to be employed with great care and precision to ensure success in litigation. Some of these actions-at-law were already in use before the Twelve Tables was enacted as law in 450 BCE. The earliest interpreters of the law or 'jurists' are said to have been members from the college of pontiffs, priests of Roman state religion. That these officials had both religious and legal functions is to be expected in a system where much of the law was unwritten custom and where a clear distinction between legal and religion norms was not maintained. Based on account by the Roman historian Livy, it is commonly said that these pontiffs, who were exclusively elected from the patrician class, exercised a monopoly over knowledge of the law (this forms part of the larger narrative about the 'struggle of the orders'). In time this is said to have caused popular discontent and may have been one of the factors which forced the patricians to submit to the creation of the Twelve Tables in which some of the more controversial aspects of Roman customary law were written down and displayed publicly for all to see. While this went some way to pleasing the plebeians, it seems clear that some areas of the law remained unclear and subject to pontifical interpretation. This may account for the existence of the popular tale of Appius Claudius, a clerk of one of these pontiffs, who stole a document containing details of the actions-at-law and published it. This broke the pontifical monopoly over the law (and presumably also over legal practice). In a related development, it is also towards the end of this period when the first 'jurist', Tiberius Coruncanius, emerges in Roman law. He is said to have been one of the first plebeian holders of the office of pontiff and was the first to provide members of the public with legal advice in public.

The pre-classical period of Roman law (c. 250-27 BCE) covers the remainder of the Roman Republic. It is a turbulent period in Roman history which opens with Rome's first attempts to expand her territories outside Italy and ends with the bloody feuding between great men and the fall of the Republic. The early years of this period were dominated by the First and Second Punic Wars against Carthage. The first of these led to the annexation of Sardinia and Corsica while the second ended with the comprehensive defeat of the Carthaginians and the destruction of their capital. The end of the Second Punic War (c. 201 BCE) not only gave Rome a much larger territory to govern, but also brought it into contact with various hostile forces abroad such as Alexander the Great and Mithridates. Domestically, social upheaval continued to dominate local politics, especially in relation to the struggle for property and wealth. This can be seen from the events surrounding the Gracchi brothers (c. 133-132 BCE) who attempted to obtain greater land rights for small farmers. For much of the second century BCE, civil strife continued within Roman territories, culminating in the Social War of 91-89 BCE. This period of strife is often referred to as 'the Roman revolution' (to use the phrase first coined by Ronald Syme in 1939). The main reason for this war lay in Rome's decision not to grant citizenship to all her allies as had been done in the past. The last century of the Roman Republic witnessed a number of important events. First, the senate became the most important legislative body even if only indirectly (by having a senate decision incorporated into a statute). Secondly, the army was transformed into a professional corps paid by the state. In a related development, the economy becomes increasingly sophisticated towards the end of the Republic with complex financial institutions such as banks emerging. The final period of the Republic, from Caesar's successes in Gaul to the Battle of Actium in 31 BCE is a well-known tale. The in-fighting of great men such as Caesar and Mark Anthony, supported by various political factions, could not be contained by temporary measures such as the creation of triumvirates, and the Republic ended.

As for the law during this period, there is a general movement away from unwritten custom towards statute law enacted initially by the council of the plebs and other *comitiae*, later through decisions of the senate. Although statute law played an important role in the second half of the Republic, few examples may be identified. It has been suggested that most of the statute law from this period was not preserved. This is perhaps an over-simplification of a more complex issue, since the transition from unwritten custom to written law does not necessarily presuppose the increased use of statute. It also fails to take account of the growing importance of praetorian law which, as will be discussed presently, came to be an important source of law during this period. Of the important legal events which occurred during this period, three deserve specific mention. First, the creation of a second praetorship in 242 BCE heralded an important change in Roman court procedure. Before, a single praetorship existed and this officer presided over courts which were exclusively available to Roman citizens and which applied Roman law using Roman procedure. By 242 BCE, a number of foreigners had settled in Roman territories and, since they were barred from using Roman law in Roman courts, a parallel system of courts evolved. This court, which was not constrained by the formalism of early Roman law and court procedure, proved so effective that by 150 BCE a *Lex Aebutia* was enacted which enabled Roman citizens to use this more flexible procedure also in Roman courts (though at first it may have been limited to certain areas of law). The enactment of this statute started a process which would eventually culminate in the replacement of the system of procedure in all Roman courts by the end of this period (the actions-at-law were specifically abolished by statute during the reign of Augustus). One of the other main legal developments which can be located in the late Republic is the *actio Publiciana*, a legal remedy introduced *c.* 67 BCE to protect possessors of land who were on their way to acquiring ownership. It is plausible that this development is in some way related to the expansion of Roman territories.

Two further legal developments deserve mention. First, the office of the praetor, created in 367 BCE and augmented by the introduction of the office of the peregrine praetor in 242 BCE, in time came to have a profound impact on the development of law. Praetors, by virtue of their office, could produce edicts, statements of principle which would govern their term in office. From *c.* 150 BCE when the civil procedure used in Roman courts became less formalised, these edicts began to have a direct impact on legal change. While in theory, the old civil law of the Romans founded on ancient customs augmented by statute continued to exist, in practice legal developments introduced by the praetor through his edict increasingly came to 'aid, supplement and correct' the civil law according to Cicero. It is often said that during this period Roman law became a 'science' (evidence of this can be seen in the appearance of concepts such as natural law and the law of nations in Roman legal sources). To some extent, this must have occurred because of the influence of Greek philosophy which is known to have exerted a formative influence over much of Roman society, especially during the second century BCE. As far as the activities of the praetor is concerned, it is important to remember that this office did not act alone. Praetors (as political officers) were often assisted by men knowledgeable about the law – jurists. Initially, jurists were mostly men from the patrician order who followed in the footsteps of Tiberius Coruncanius by providing citizens with legal advice for free. Other notable jurists of the period include Sextus Aelius who is said to have attempted to systematise Roman law by dividing it into three parts, Quintus Mucius Scaevola who divided the law into categories, and Aquilius Gallus who wrote commentaries on the law. By the end of this period, there were many jurists in Rome and the provinces. These individuals were no longer solely from patrician stock. Rather, they came from a wide variety of social backgrounds and practised law in return for payment. Cicero commented on the activities of the jurists. Jurists wrote learned treatises on the law, taught students using an informal system of apprenticeship, and advised officials and clients regarding the law. Although jurists were important in the development of Roman law, it must be remembered that clients were not represented by jurists in court. They were represented by advocates like Cicero, individuals trained in rhetoric whose task it was to convince a lay judge of the truth of their client's case using the techniques of rhetoric.

Politically, the classical period (*c.* 27 BCE-284 CE) was one of consolidation when the eastern and western borders of Roman Empire assumed a regular form, although this did not end periodic skirmishes. The transition from Republic to Empire, chiefly owing to the efforts of Octavian (later renamed Augustus) is a master-class in political manoeuvring. While maintaining the notion of a Republic headed by 'the first among the equals', Augustus took great care to preserve much of the republican constitutional machinery such as the senate and the voting assemblies (to prevent stirring up the anti-monarchical feelings of the Roman populace). Under the successors of Augustus, collectively known as the Julio-Claudian dynasty, the final vestiges of republicanism were removed so that by the end of the first century CE there was little power left in the republican assemblies to challenge the position of the emperor. Under the successors to the Julian-Claudian dynasty, the Flavian dynasty, the emperor's power was consolidated further and greater links were forged between Rome and her provinces. The Severan emperors, successors to the Flavians, continued this work until *c.* 235 CE when the last of them, Alexander Severus, was murdered. This event triggered a period of great instability, commonly referred to as the crisis of the third century. Between 235 and 284 CE not only was Rome almost continuously involved in skirmishes with the Goths on the Danube frontier, but old hostilities between the Romans and the Parthians in Asia Minor flared up again. There was great economic upheaval, and taxes had to be raised to fund military spending. It was a time of many emperors and pretenders, all of whom reigned for short periods. Order was not restored until 284 CE with the accession of the Emperor Diocletian.

The classical period represents the high point of Roman legal development, but relatively few important statutes from this period can be identified. Of these, the majority date from the beginning of the period, which suggests that statute law (as approved and enacted by the old popular voting assemblies) declined as the emperor and his bureaucracy grew in importance as a direct source of law. The most noteworthy of these statutes were the Augustan marriage laws (*Leges Iuliae* of 18-17 BCE; *Lex Aelia Sentia* and *Lex Papia Poppaea* of 4 CE) which set out to promote marriage by criminalising adultery and imposing various social and financial fines on cohabiters. This set of laws also curtailed the number of slaves an owner could free at any one time. Three further legal innovations deserve specific mention. In 52 CE a senatorial decree (the *senatusconsultum Claudianum*) determined the legal status of children born from a male slave and a freedwoman, while in 135 CE an imperial decree by order of Hadrian set in motion the codification of the Praetorian Edict. An imperial decree of 212 CE (the *Constitutio Antoniniana*) deserves specific mention. Issued by order of the Emperor Antoninus Pius, it granted Roman citizenship to most of the free inhabitants of the Roman Empire. The legal significance of this measure should not be underestimated. Whereas before, Roman citizenship determined whether a person was entitled to use Roman law in a Roman court, this edict extended the use of Roman law throughout the Empire. In parts of the Empire such as Egypt, where a sophisticated and well-developed legal culture had existed prior to the annexation by Rome, the effect of this decree must have been to intensify the existing legal pluralism.

Attempts by successive emperors to consolidate their own power at the expense of the existing republican constitutional assemblies had a noticeable effect on the law. Thus, from Augustus onwards, the importance of these assemblies waned to the extent that by 200 CE, the senate was little more than a sounding board for the wishes of the emperor. The other main sources of law, juristic writing and praetorian edicts were also affected by this development. The Praetorian Edict, which by the start of this period was a sizeable document that incumbent praetors were expected to adopt without much alteration, was eventually redacted into its final form during the first half of the second century CE by order of the Emperor Hadrian. The demise of this source of law is not difficult to comprehend. First, it did not sit well with the increasing centralising tendencies of the emperor and his bureaucracy. Secondly, the Edict existed in the context of a specific type of court procedure, the formulary procedure which had originally evolved in the court of the peregrine praetor. With the advent of the Empire, the formulary procedure was increasingly being replaced by a more centralised, bureaucratic procedure developed in special imperial tribunals. Although the formulary procedure was not officially abolished until the mid-fourth century CE, its use was increasingly restricted both in imperial tribunals and in the provinces. This must have affected the way in which the Praetorian Edict was used as a source of law.

As far as the works of the jurists are concerned, the thriving independent legal culture of the late Republic was replaced by a culture of regulation (the *ius respondendi*). Augustus introduced a system of official regulation whereby some jurists were granted the right to give authoritative responses. It is not known what criteria were employed for the award of this privilege: it has been suggested that it may have been given as token of political allegiance. Whatever the criteria may have been, the granting of this right gave a jurist more prestige and it also gave such an opinion more weight in law during litigation. In fact, if all jurists who had this right and who were consulted on a point of law were in agreement, the court was bound to follow it. Although the jurists continued their activities as outlined by Cicero, they began to be organised into factions or schools. Legal texts mention at least two schools, the Proculians and Sabinians, who held different views (sometimes inspired by philosophy) on points of law. Apart from the established activities, jurists also increasingly began to be appointed to imperial councils advising the emperor on matters of law. One may also assume that they were increasingly employed in the imperial bureaucracy and that this ultimately led to the demise of the profession of the jurist. The Emperor Hadrian ended the practice of granting the right to give authoritative responses to individual jurists and began to give imperial enactments in his own name. This led to a decline in the profession; and no named jurist is known after 284 CE, presumably because they were all subsumed into the imperial bureaucracy.

Compared to their republican counterparts, much more is known about the jurists of the classical period. The reasons for this are twofold. First, the works of thirty-eight of the most prominent jurists who held the right to give authoritative responses were anthologised in the Digest, a legal encyclopaedia which formed part of the compilation of Roman law by order of the sixth-century Emperor Justinian. Secondly, one of these classical works by an otherwise unknown jurist called Gaius was redis-covered largely intact as a palimpsest during the course of the nineteenth century. This book is unique. Not only is it the only largely intact work from the classical period which has been preserved, but it also provides a unique glimpse into a teaching manual of the classical period. Gaius was also clearly interested in legal history as much of the law discussed by him is placed in its historical context.

After the death of the Emperor Alexander Severus in 235 CE, the Roman Empire was virtually constantly under attack from the Parthians in Asia Minor and the Germanic tribes on the Rhine and Danube frontiers for a period of fifty years. This had various consequences. Emperors tended to reign for short periods and were quickly deposed, often by their own armies who found them to be ineffectual. Increased military expen-diture caused economic decline, higher taxes and inflation. Prolonged warfare led to food shortages and caused popular unrest. It was also during this period (owing to military threats from all sides) that the seat of the Roman Empire started to shift eastward. The decline was partially arrested by the promotion of Diocletian to the imperial throne in 284 CE. Dio-cletian had in fact been involved in imperial politics for some time, but it was only after he became sole emperor in 284 CE that he began to implement significant changes. An able military tactician and bureaucrat, Diocletian addressed the problem of the size of the Empire by dividing it into two administrative units each governed by a co-emperor and assisted by his deputy. This constitutional division, the Tetrarchy, solved many of the practical problems created by the size of the Empire. It is also conventionally seen as the start of the Dominate, an increasingly bureau-cratic period in Roman history characterised by a large state, in which the emperor and his bureaucracy became the sole lawgiver.

Although the succession to the imperial throne after Diocletian was troubled, one figure, Constantine, emerged victorious. Constantine's reign is noteworthy for a number of reasons. An able administrator like his predecessor, Constantine continued the programme of bureaucratic reforms to stabilise the Empire. Since by this time the position of the emperor at the head of the Roman state had been firmly established, the civil service was expanded and the role of the senate was downgraded. Arguably the most notable achievement for which Constantine has become known to posterity is his attempt to end the persecution of Christians which had begun during the first century CE. Thus, in 313 CE, through the Edict of Milan, Constantine decreed an end to the official state-sanctioned prosecution of Christians. Much has been written about Constantine's own conversion to Christianity, but it is not clear whether an Empire-wide conversion occurred during his reign. Certainly by 391 CE, during the reign of Theodosius I, Christianity had become the official religion of the Roman Empire. Constantine also tried to improve relations between church and state and to preserve unity within the church by calling together the main church leaders to the council of Nicea in 325 CE. His other notable achievement was the capital investment in the city of Constantinople (later Byzantium) on the Bosphorus, another indication of the decline in the importance of Rome. Following the death of Constantine in 337 CE, two years of strife over his succession followed. This was eventually resolved by the election of Theodosius I. During his reign other cities such as Milan and Ravenna became increasingly important.

The Dominate, as the term suggests, is characterised by a centralised approach to government and the law. All other sources of law declined in importance compared to the imperial bureaucracy and the emperor as the primary source of law. This reflects the changing nature of the emperor as the head of the Roman state. He is no longer seen as first among equals, but as the sole anointed ruler of the Roman Empire by divine right. Evidence of the decline of other sources of law in favour of imperial law is visible in a number of areas. Although the formulary procedure was still technically available to litigants in Roman courts, it had long since been abandoned for (or merged into) a more bureaucratic form of procedure known as the *cognitio* in which judges were salaried officials in the employment of the state. The formulary process was not officially abolished until 342 CE, but it must be assumed that it had fallen into disuse well before that time. Another way in which the emperor asserted his authority over the administration of justice was through the formalisation of a system of appeals (and thus also a hierarchy of courts). One further point deserves mention. After the conversion to Christianity, bishops slowly acquired jurisdiction over certain aspects of (mostly family) law. This led to the rise of bishop's courts and the slow fragmentation of state jurisdiction into secular and religious spheres.

As far as private law based on statutes and the writings of jurists are concerned, there is evidence of the 'vulgarisation' of the law. Since independent juristic activity seems to have ceased during the third century CE, it became necessary for the courts to evolve a doctrine to deal with the existing body of jurists' writings. This is to be found in the so-called Law of Citations of 426 CE, a piece of legislation regulating the use of the sources of the classical period in a court of law. The works of five of the greatest jurists of the classical period (Gaius, Ulpian, Paulus, Papinian and Modestinus) were seen as sources, and these were applied according to rules laid down in the statute. This mechanical application of juristic authority is a far cry from the intellectual vibrancy of the classical period. On the other hand, perhaps it was merely a pragmatic solution to the thorny issue of legal authority in late antiquity. Given the absence of independent juristic activity and the increasing bureaucratisation of the law, attempts at codification were inevitable. The product of this process was the Theodosian Code of 438 CE, compiled by order of the Emperor Theodosius II. An incomplete version of the text has been preserved from which it has been concluded that the Theodosian Code was based on two earlier unofficial codes of law known as the Codes of Gregorian and Hermogenian respectively. These have not been preserved and their content is unknown except for an index page. The Theodosian Code is largely concerned with imperial law from the reign of Hadrian until Theodosius II. It deals with public law and, although reference is made to a proposed future project on private law, this was never undertaken.

The later history of the Roman Empire is inextricably linked to that of the advent of the middle ages in Western Europe. In 476 CE the puppet emperor of the Western Empire, Romulus Augustulus, was deposed by a 'barbarian' chieftain, Odoacer. This event, although hardly significant in its own right, signalled the end of the Roman Empire in Western Europe. Except for a brief period of reconquest during the reign of the Byzantine Emperor Justinian, Italy became the home of the Ostrogoths (later defeated by the Lombards), one of the Germanic tribes against which the Roman had fought for so long. In the east, the boundaries established by Diocletian between the Eastern and Western Roman Empire now became the formal boundary between the Byzantine Empire and the 'barbarian' West. As the successor to the Roman Empire, the Byzantine Empire would in time produce one of the greatest figures of late antiquity, the Emperor Justinian, whose attempts to restore the glory of Roman law through an ambitious project of compilation would have a long-lasting influence of the laws of Europe. Byzantine civilisation proved remarkably resilient, its empire lasting until it was defeated by the Ottomans in 1453.

*

The potted history of Roman law set out above demonstrates that for each period under discussion the law was said to derive from certain sources (custom, statute, writings of the jurists). In this respect, Roman law is no different from a modern legal system in which the law may also be said to be derived from a finite number of agreed sources (in civil-law systems mostly statute and in some also precedent, i.e. decided court cases). As mentioned above in relation to the classical period, the main sources of Roman law during this period were (in no specific order) statute law, the Praetorian Edict, the writings of the jurists and, towards the end of this period, imperial law. Let us look at each of these in turn.

With a few exceptions, Roman statutes tend to deal with specific issues rather than as a general restatement of the law. Statute law is more prevalent during the Republic than during the Empire (when the emperor and his bureaucracy became the dominant source of law), but many of the republican statutes remained in force and therefore need to be taken into account when constructing the law of the classical period. It is also important to consider who could make statute law and the nature of the legislative process. Most Roman statutes attested in literary or epigraphic form have been collected in C.G. Bruns, *Fontes Iuris Romani Antiqui*, 5th edn, ed. Th. Mommsen (Freiburg in Breisgau 1887), augmented by S. Riccobono et al. (eds) *Fontes Iuris Romani Anteiustiniani*, 3 vols (Florence 1941-3). The most recent work on Roman statutes is M. Crawford (ed.) *Roman Statutes*, 2 vols (London 1996), which contains a thorough text-critical analysis of many statutes along with detailed commentary. Since the publication of Crawford's book, a number of new statutes have come to light, such as the *Lex Irnitana* (a town charter from Spain) and the *Lex Rivi Hiberiensis* (an irrigation decree also from Spain). These have been edited and published in the *Journal of Roman Studies* and may be accessed there.

Roman statutes tend to contain highly formalised language. Take the following example from the *Lex Iulia de maritandis ordinibus* from the reign of Augustus. The aim of this piece of legislation was to prohibit marriages between people of different (read: unsuitable) classes:

Whoever is <or shall be> a senator or whoever is or shall be a son of any of them or a grandson through a son or a great-grandson through <a grandson> born to a son, none of them, knowingly with wrongful deceit, is to have as fiancée or wife a freedwoman <or someone> who herself is or shall have been an actress or whose father or mother is or shall have been an actor or actress. ...
[translation: Crawford II, 807]

The drafters of this passage were influenced by the idea of patriarchy descending through the male line (*agnatio*), an important principle in the law of persons. Furthermore, the law was designed to catch a wide category of potential unsuitable marriages by extending the ban to the third-generation descendants of senators (i.e. families of a certain standing). The law set to punish only those who had contravened it on purpose ('knowingly or with wrongful deceit'). Finally, it is worth noting that the class of unsuitables included both former slaves since freed as well as those who practised professions that upper-class Romans regarded as vulgar, such as acting.

When assessing statutes such as this one, two points need to be borne in mind. First, Roman statutes had a very narrow purpose, namely to change the law on a specific point. It is therefore always good to establish what the law on this point stated prior to the enactment of the legislation and to attempt to work out (using literary and other evidence) what the motivation for the change was. Secondly, the Romans tended to interpret statutes conservatively. Since it is likely that the Roman jurists would have commented on this piece of legislation, a good strategy is to establish which jurists wrote specifically on this law (this can be ascertained using F. Schulz, *Roman Legal Science* (Oxford 1954)) and to ascertain whether any of these works (or sections from them) were incorporated into the Digest of Justinian. By looking at juristic writing on this legislation, it is possible to obtain a sense, not only of juristic thought on the law, but also of its engagement with legal practice.

Our second main source of law for the classical period is the Praetorian Edict. As mentioned above, praetors (who were in charge of the administration of justice in Rome) produced an annual edict in which they set out the new legal grounds on which they were prepared to grant legal relief. By the advent of the Principate, successive praetors had been following this tradition for a century and a half, and it had been established that praetors were bound by the Edict (possibly owing to the transgressions of Verres) since the first century BCE. The Edict contained a list of *formulae* of actions created by successive praetors who, through custom, had come to adopt the edicts of their predecessors while weeding out failed remedies. It also contained the *formulae* for other forms of summary relief such as interdicts. By studying the structure of the Edict as redacted into its final form during the reign of the Emperor Hadrian, it is possible to ascertain when certain remedies were introduced by the praetor into Roman law and possibly also in response to which factors. A reconstruction of the Edict has been attempted by O. Lenel, *Das Edictum Perpetuum*, 2nd improved edn (Leipzig 1907). Let us take an example. The *formula* of the action on letting and hiring (*actio locati*) states:

> Whereas Aulus Agerius [the plaintiff] let to Numerius Negidius [the defendant] the plot of land in question which is the object of the lawsuit, whatever on those grounds the defendant ought to do or give to the plaintiff in accordance with good faith, I instruct you, oh judge, to condemn the defendant or if it cannot be proven to acquit him. [translation: mine, from Lenel §111]

Letting and hiring is one of a group of four contracts known as 'consensual', because they could be created purely by the consent of the parties on a certain range of issues. As we can see from this *formula*, good faith was an important principle in assessing the amount of the condemnation. We will return to this issue in our discussion of actions in Chapter 4.

Since the Praetorian Edict was a public document which was displayed in the forum, this *formula* would have been visible to potential litigants wishing to sue on the basis of a breach of contract in letting and hiring. It provided the framework in which the parties had to state their claim in law. During the first stage of the lawsuit, in front of the praetor, this *formula* would be adapted to take account of the specific case of the parties. Both parties would have an opportunity to add claims and defences to the *formula* until such time as they (and the praetor) were content that all the legal issues had been set out in the claim. It was usually in advance of this stage that the parties would have sought advice from jurists. Once both the parties and the praetor were content about the *formula*, a judge could be appointed and the lawsuit could progress to the second stage.

The Praetorian Edict is a useful source for reconstructing classical Roman law. Not only does it show the technicalities of the formulary procedure, but it also demonstrates the relationship between legal theory and legal practice. The praetorship was a political office and many of the holders of this office had no legal expertise. It must therefore be assumed that the technical nature of the *formulae* contained in the Edict was created by the jurists who advised the praetor. This, in turn, raises interesting questions about the relationship between the jurists and legal practice and the Roman conception of 'law', since the praetor was not technically a lawmaker who could change the *ius civile*. Furthermore, many of the jurists wrote commentaries on the Edict (Ulpian, for one) (F. Schulz, *Roman Legal Science* (Oxford 1954) provides a good overview). By studying their comments on specific aspects of the Edict, it is possible to gain some insight into their methods of analysis as well as their interpretation of these *formulae* during the classical period.

By far the most abundant source of information about the classical period comes from the works of the Roman jurists. Let us first look at the most complete example of such a work, the Institutes of Gaius. This textbook for law students written during the second half of the second century CE by an unknown jurist from the eastern provinces of the Roman Empire is the only (nearly) complete example of juristic writing from the classical period. As an example of juristic writing, it stands squarely within the tradition of Roman legal writing in which the jurists of this period excelled. The book has a number of interesting features. First, it is conceptually divided into three sections, namely, persons, things and actions (a threefold division much discussed by modern Romanists owing to its lasting impact on Western jurisprudence). Secondly, since it was written before the widespread grant of Roman citizenship to nearly all free inhabitants living within the boundaries of the Empire in 212 CE, it has a specific focus and only really deals with Roman law, in the sense of the *ius civile*, available to Roman citizens. Gaius pays little attention to the legal position of non-citizens living in Roman territories and who did not have access to Roman civil law. Furthermore, it is clear from the content of the work that Gaius was interested in the history of Roman law. He frequently mentions institutions and rituals which, by his time, must have long fallen into disuse. Thus the Institutes can also be used to gain insights into earlier periods of Roman legal history. Finally, it is known that Gaius was a follower of the Sabinian school of jurists. During the course of the classical period, most Roman jurists had begun to affiliate themselves with one of two 'schools', the Proculians or the Sabinians. The difference between them is not altogether clear, with some modern scholars arguing that the differences were philosophical while others think that one 'school' had republican sympathies and the other imperial sympathies. Be that as it may, Gaius, who is known to have been a follower of the Sabinian school, nearly always sides with them in matters of legal controversy. Since we have more evidence of Gaius' reasoning in these matters than that of the other Roman jurists, he provides us with useful information on the differences between these two 'schools'.

The Institutes of Gaius is conventionally cited in the form Inst.Gai.III, 4 (= book III, paragraph 4). W.M. Gordon and O.F. Robinson's *The Institutes of Gaius* (London 1988) is a modern critical edition of the Latin text together with an English translation. Let us take an example:

Wills properly made may be invalidated if the testator changes his mind. But it is clear that a will does not become invalid merely because the testator wants to rescind it. Why, even if he cuts the thread holding it together it is still valid by state law [read civil law]. Indeed, even if he destroys or burns the will, what was written in it is no less valid, although proof of what that was may be difficult (Inst.Gai.II, 151) [translation: Gordon/Robinson]

This passage is concerned with the law of testate succession (i.e. inheritance based on a valid will in which the final wishes of the deceased have been recorded), which we will discuss in greater detail in Chapter 3. To the Romans, this branch of law was classified as forming part of the law of 'things', inheritance being the way in which one acquired ownership of 'things'. This passage contains a number of interesting points. It provides us with some information about the physical make-up of Roman wills (a scroll containing writing and sealed with a thread to preserve the confidentiality of the contents). However, the main legal point Gaius makes here is that a testator is entitled to change his mind after the will has been made. Notice that the 'rule of law' which Gaius explains to his students here is one that has grown organically out of Roman civil law. Its authority does not lie in any statute, but has grown out of Roman legal custom augmented by legal practice. No doubt the examples of the invalidation of a will have also arisen out of practice. How do we know that Gaius' view on this matter accurately represents the law at the time when the Institutes was produced? First, there is no indication from the passage that he is discussing law which has been altered. Secondly, by comparing this passage to others from the classical period as well as to examples of legal practice which have been preserved, it becomes possible to draw conclusions about whether the law expressed here is current.

Our second category of juristic works is not in the same format as that of Gaius. The reason for this is that they were anthologised during the sixth century CE by the compilers of Justinian's great project to create a manageable *corpus* of Roman law. The work into which these books were redacted is called the Digest. It contains our main source of information on juristic literature, not only of the 'classical' period, but also of the state of the law during the reign of Justinian (an English translation may be found in A. Watson (ed.) *The Digest of Justinian*, rev. edn, 4 vols (Philadelphia 2008)). Let us consider how the Digest was put together. A commission of seventeen men was instructed to review the books of thirty-eight jurists of the classical period. These were the most important jurists of their day, awarded the *ius respondendi* (the right to give authoritative responses) during their lifetime. Gaius was one of them. Two thousand books by these thirty-eight jurists were reviewed by the commission and redacted into thematic titles (e.g. on sale, on marriage). Within each title, snippets of texts from these original books were arranged in an order that reflected the working practices of the commission. Let us take an example:

> D.23.2.31 Ulpian, *Lex Iulia et Papia*, book 6. Where a senator is given imperial permission to marry a freedwoman, she will be his lawful wife. [translation: A. Watson]

This snippet of text, which in the Digest may be found in the title 'formation of marriage' (D.23.2) was taken from a volume on the *Lex Iulia et Papia* (book 6) by a jurist called Ulpian. The compilers of the Digest included the provenance of every text snippet and it is therefore possible to attribute every text to a specific author (of the thirty-eight jurists whose work make up the Digest) as well as to a specific work by that author. These facts are particularly important for at least two reasons. First, by identifying the author, it allows us to place the snippet in time. Ulpian, a frequently cited jurist in the Digest, lived during the third century CE. Knowing that this statement came from the third century CE permits us to draw conclusions about the state of the law during that period. Secondly, by identifying the book from which this was taken, it is possible to draw further conclusions about the law.

This text was taken from a work by Ulpian on the *Lex Iulia et Papia*. Jurists wrote many different kinds of works: commentaries on statutes, collections of legal advice, theoretical works (for an account of the different types, see F. Schulz, *Roman Legal Science* (Oxford 1954)). Given the title of this work, it was most likely a commentary on the above-mentioned statute. We have come across this statute before in our discussion of statute law, where we saw that its aim was to ban intermarriage between 'unsuitable' and suitable people. Knowing this, we may therefore conclude, looking at this statement by Ulpian, that the effect of the statute could be avoided by obtaining permission from the emperor to marry a freedwoman. This also gives us some information about the relationship between the existing law and imperial innovation. Finally, given that not only the title of the original book from which the snippet was taken has been included, but also the book from which it was taken, it would theoretically be possible to reconstruct the original works from the snippets in the Digest. These reconstructions may prove useful in assessing the original context in which a statement was made (by looking at the paragraph above and below it). An attempt at reconstructing these works have been made by Otto Lenel in a multi-volume work entitled *Palingenesia Iuris Civilis* (Leipzig 1899).

Two complications surrounding these texts remain. First, the format of these works by the classical jurists (which by the time of the compilation of the Digest must already have been nearly three centuries old) and whether they had been standardised by the time of the compilation are unknown. In second place, the compilers made certain changes to the texts in order to reflect the law of the Justinianic period (i.e. the scored out references to institutions which had become obsolete), but it is generally assumed that most of these changes were largely cosmetic.

Our other main source of Roman law of the classical period is imperial 'constitutions' collected in another part of Justinian's compilation of Roman law, the Codex Iustinianus (the best English-language translation is the one by Fred Blume available online via the website of the George W. Hopper Library of the University of Wyoming). To understand this form of law and its effect on existing law, a few observations about the changing nature of law during the Principate is required. During the Republic, statutory convention dictated that a statute could only be passed once a certain legislative procedure had been concluded in the voting assemblies. The decisions of the senate did not have the force of statute unless they were incorporated in a statute. With the advent of the Principate, the enactment of statute law by the voting assemblies slowly declined in favour of new forms of legislation. From the reign of Hadrian the decisions of the senate had the force of law, a state of affairs which continued until the Dominate; thereafter the 'constitutions' of the emperor, made via his bureaucracy, increasingly came to have the force of law. The exact basis for the emperor's legislative ability is unclear, but it stands to reason that as the position of the emperor as head of the Roman state grew stronger it became easier to justify the legislative basis of these 'constitutions'. This term is used as a collective to describe three forms of imperial law. The first of these, edicts, referred to the emperor's ability, as a supreme magistrate, to issue legally binding directives (or edicts). These were in theory perpetual until altered by a later emperor. The second were missives to imperial governors and other officials. They were known as *mandata* and there is some debate as to whether they count as law or not. In theory they applied only as long as the emperor was in office. The final form appeared in two versions. Imperial decrees (*decreta*) were instances in which the emperor ruled in a legal dispute brought before him. Such rulings were perpetually binding and changed the law. The other version, *rescripta*, is most commonly found in the Codex Iustinianus. They were written answers on points of law given in response to petitions from individuals or legal officials. They were binding and changed the law. Let us take an example.

> C.4.65.3 The Emperor Antoninus to Flavius Callimorphus. You should not be expelled, against your will, from the room which you say you hired, if you pay the rent to the owner of an apartment house, unless such owner proves that it is necessary for his own use, or that he wants to improve it, or that you conducted yourself badly in the rented room. (6 January 214 CE) [translation: F. Blume]

Like the Digest, these 'constitutions' were organised into titles by subject (this one is taken from the title on letting and hiring) (C.4.65). Within each title, they were arranged chronologically from earliest to latest. The text provides the name of the author and the name of the petitioner (often an unknown person) as well as the date and often also the place of promulgation. These snippets of information are important because they allow us to date the fragment and thus enable us to draw more general conclusions about the development of the law. When dealing with imperial 'constitutions' these need to be compared to juristic law on any given point to see whether the law was changed by the emperor acting through his bureaucracy.

Two further sources of Roman law may be mentioned. The first of these are *negotia*, written records of legal practice preserved on papyrus or wax tablets (most of which are recorded in Riccobono (ed.), vol. 3). In the last fifty years, a number of these have come to light, providing us with exciting new information about legal practice. Take the following example from the Sulpicii archive, a collection of financial documents belonging to the Sulpicii banker family found in Puteoli.

> TPSulp. 45. I, Diognetus, slave of Gaius Novius Cypaerus, have written: By order of my master Cypaerus and in his presence I have leased to Hesychus, slave of Tiberius Iulius Evenus, imperial freedman, Bunker No. 12 on the middle level of the publicly-owned Bassian warehouses in Puteoli, ... [translation: Jones, p. 95]

At face value this document records a contract of letting and hiring. Its importance, however, lies in the fact that slaves are transacting on behalf of their masters. Diognetus 'with authorisation and ... in his presence' is clearly intending to bind his master fully to the agreement. Thus, by looking at these documents, it is possible to form a better appreciation of law in action and how the abstract rules of Roman law discussed by the jurists in their works applied to real-life situations. Apart from these, there are a vast number of papyri which record legal transactions from the period of the Roman occupation of North Africa. Although these are a fascinating source, it should be borne in mind that Roman provinces like Egypt already had a sophisticated indigenous legal system before they were annexed by the Romans and that in many cases the Roman authorities were content to allow a form of legal pluralism to exist whereby local courts were left to apply local laws. Thus, in assessing whether the law as described in these documents may be said to be 'Roman' one needs to take account of the existence of local laws.

Apart from these, there also exists a vast body of Latin literature spanning the classical period which could be used to draw conclusions about Roman law. Authors like Horace, Cicero, Pliny the Elder, Pliny the Younger, Quintilian and Celsus are well known to scholars of Roman law for the information their writings provide (most Latin works may be found in standardised form in the Loeb series and Greek works in the Teubner series). Two things need to be borne in mind when evaluating statements from Latin literature. First, each of these authors wrote in a specific genre (philosophical treatises, historical works, moralistic works) and their statements about the law therefore have to be seen in context of the type of work. Thus, when Cicero comments that law is a discipline with which you occupy yourself in old age, we should not take this at face value, but merely as a quip about the usefulness of the law to a professional advocate. In second place, it should not be forgotten that these authors were not professional jurists with a scientific interest in the law. Thus their statements are sometimes incomplete or incorrect and show only an aspect of the law that they wished to reveal in the larger context of their narrative.

Suggested further reading

The following works contain useful overviews of Roman legal history. They may be used to obtain more detailed information about the main developments outlined above.

Frier, B.W. *The Rise of the Roman Jurists* (Princeton NJ 1985)
Mousourakis, G. *A Legal History of Rome* (London 2007)
Riggsby, A. *Roman Law and the Legal World of the Romans* (Cambridge 2010)

Robinson, O.F. *The Sources of Roman Law: Problems and Methods for Ancient Historians* (London 1997)

Tellegen-Couperus, O.E. *A Short History of Roman Law* (London 1993)

Watson, A. *Lawmaking in the Later Roman Republic* (Oxford 1974)

Chapter 2

Persons

The law of persons and family is an important component of the threefold division of Roman private law set out in the Institutes of Gaius. In a legal order such as that of the Romans , this branch of law fulfilled an important function. Strictly speaking, the phrase 'the law of persons and family' is a modern rendition of a Roman legal category. To the Roman jurists, it was the law which applied to 'persons' (*persona* in Latin, which means 'mask'), the family being a legal construct (albeit a very important one, as we shall see) of 'persons' for the purposes of the law. This focus on the individual can be seen from the following statement by Gaius:

> Inst.Gai.I.8. The whole of the law we observe relates either to persons or to things or to actions. Let us first consider persons. [translation: Handouts]

There is a person-focused quality to the ordering of these concepts. Central to the law was the 'person', followed by his things and thereafter his actions. But who was a 'person' for the purposes of the law? In Roman law, which was a patriarchal system, the most important 'person' in law was the head of the household (the *paterfamilias*), since it was from his domestic power over the *familia*, which had arisen during the time of Romulus, that most of the law of persons and family developed. As we shall see, the head of the household was the main actor in this branch of law and had the most complete 'status' for the purposes of the law.

Prior to 212 CE, when most free inhabitants of the Roman Empire were granted citizenship by an imperial decree of the Emperor Caracalla, Roman law applied only to those who held Roman citizenship (or who had been granted a special dispensation). In the context of the law of persons and family, therefore, the Roman legal mind made a connection between *persona* and citizenship. To phrase it differently, the Roman law of persons and family applied only to those people who were regarded by the legal order as 'persons', and to be regarded as such one needed to hold Roman citizenship. When surveying Roman legal texts on this matter, it is clear that the term 'person' for the purposes of the law primarily referred to a human being (or a natural person, as we would say in modern law). Although some clubs and societies were treated in law as if they were 'persons' (juristic persons in modern law) in the sense that they (like a person) could litigate on behalf of their members, these were not classified as such in the law of persons and family and thus need not concern us here.

Not all people were deemed 'persons' for the purposes of Roman law. As mentioned above, before 212 CE Roman law linked personality and citizenship. Thus, anyone who did not have Roman citizenship did not benefit from this branch of the law. One group of human beings in particular was completely excluded from the working of the law of persons and family: slaves. A unique duality exists in relation to the status of slaves in Roman law. On the one hand, they are described by Gaius as *personae* (no doubt reflecting the many different shades of meaning of this term), but on the other hand they were completely excluded from the operation of the law of persons and treated as objects (movable property, as we shall see in Chapter 3) which could be sold or bartered. The exclusion of slaves from the ambit of the law of persons and family can be seen from Gaius' statement in which he sets out the primary division:

Inst.Gai.I.9. The primary division of the law of persons is that all men are either free or slaves. [translation: Handouts]

Following this statement about the division, Gaius only really deals with free Roman citizens in the context of his discussion of the Roman law of persons and family. Slaves are rarely mentioned and then only to the extent that they affect the rights of citizens (e.g. through their wrongdoing for which the owner was legally liable). It is clear that slaves existed in a grey area between a 'person' and a 'thing' for the purposes of law. One thing is clear, though, slaves had very limited access to the law of persons and family. This is why Ulpian states that:

D.50.17.209 (Ulpian, *Lex Iulia et Papia*, book 4). We can say that enslavement is almost like death. [translation: Handouts]

In a certain sense, this was true. Being a slave meant that the entire law of persons and family was unavailable to them. They had no rights (to use modern terminology) under Roman private law, as Ulpian observes:

D.50.17.32 (Ulpian, Sabinus, book 43). As far as the civil law is concerned, slaves have no rights but this is not true for natural law since where natural law is involved, all men are equal. [translation: Handouts]

By becoming a slave, one lost liberty, the principal factor distinguishing a person from an object. Liberty, combined with citizenship and your place in the *familia*, were grouped together by the Roman jurists under the heading of 'legal status' (*caput* in Latin). 'Legal status' was not fixed, but could change with one's circumstances. Take the following statement by the third-century jurist, Paul:

D.4.5.11 (Paul, Sabinus, book 2). There are three kinds of change of status (*capitis deminutio*), the greatest (*maxima*), the middle (*media*) and the least (*minima*) since there are three things we have – liberty, citizenship and family. So when we lose all of these, that is liberty and citizenship and family, this is held to amount to *capitis deminutio maxima*. When we lose citizenship but keep our liberty this is *capitis deminutio media*. When we keep both liberty and citizenship but change our family position, this is *capitis deminutio minima*. [translation: Handouts]

This meant that a person's status and thus his legal personality essentially operated on a sliding scale between two extremes of 'person' and 'thing'.

The fundamental distinction drawn by the jurist Gaius in his textbook is between those who are free and those who are slaves. The main sources of slaves in the classical period of Roman law were prisoners of war who were sold at slave auctions conducted throughout the Empire and children born from slave mothers who became the property of the owner of the slave. Occasionally, free Romans were also condemned as a severe punishment, usually for committing a crime, but these were the exceptions rather than the rule. Take the following written account of a sale for a slave from Egypt:

Agathos Daemon, the Son of Dionysius and Hermione, who resides in the city of Oxyrhynchus, by this document acknowledges to Gaius Julius Germanus, son of Gaius Julius Domitianus, that he accepts as valid the handwritten sales contract which they made concerning the female slave Dioscorous, about twenty-five years old and without distinguishing marks [i.e. scars]. Julius Germanus took possession of her from Agathos Daemon just as she was. She is nonreturnable, except for epilepsy or external claim. The price was 1200 drachmas of silver which Agathos Daemon received in full from Julius Germanus when the handwritten sales contract was made out. For this amount Julius Germanus paid the sales tax on the aforementioned slave. A warranty on this slave has been given by Agathos Daemon according to all claims made in the sale contract. (P.Oxy. 95) [translation: Shelton §200]

Notice how in this contract of sale, the parties took great care to identify the slave and to state her age and distinguishing marks. This served to identify the object of sale as required by law. Also, notice how the requirements of the law have been included as contractual terms (nonreturnable except for epilepsy or external claim). I will return to this matter in more detail in my discussion of the law of contracts.

The Roman law of slavery is unique for at least two reasons. First, the Romans enshrined the position of the slave in law. They did not need to do so: many ancient societies of the same period practised slavery without giving it legal foundation. Nor did anyone really ask them to justify it legally. The discussions concerning the legal foundations of slavery are most probably related to the rise of concepts such as natural law during the classical period. Secondly, Roman slavery was not a permanent state. Roman law provided mechanisms for release from slavery in the form of manumission – ceremonies which had to be conducted officially to release the slave from his servile state. Take the following extract from a letter written by Quintus to his brother Marcus, the great Roman orator Cicero regarding the latter's faithful slave Tiro:

My dear Marcus, with regard to Tiro, I swear by my hope to see you, and my son Cicero, and little Tullia, and your son, that you gave me the very greatest pleasure when you decided that he, who did not deserve this bad fortune, should be our friend rather than our slave. (Cicero, *Ad familiares* 16.16) [translation: Sheldon §227] (Compare the example of manumission recorded in a Roman will quoted in section 3.3 below)

The consequence of such a release depended on the way in which it had been done. On the one hand an official manumission could result in the slave acquiring a new status under Roman law (that of citizen), on the other hand an informal mode of manumission might give him only lesser rights (the *Lex Aelia Sentia* of 4 CE, for example, stated that only slaves manumitted using the official procedures and which were over a certain age were acquired Roman citizenship after manumission. Similarly, the *Lex Iunia Norbana* of 19 CE granted those who had been freed informally only the status of *Latini*). The owner's freedom to manumit slaves formally, thereby granting them citizenship, was curtailed during the Principate when Augustus introduced the *Lex Fufia Caninia* in 2 BCE, a statute which prevented owners from freeing too many slaves by way of a will, thereby swelling the ranks of the populace.

The owner of the slave had extensive power over the slave. Take the following statement by Gaius:

> Inst.Gai.I.52. Slaves are in the power (*potestas*) of their masters. This power derives from the law of nations (*ius gentium*), since it is observable among all nations alike that masters have the power of life and death over their slaves and whatever is acquired by the slave is acquired for his master. [translation: Handouts]

Three things are noteworthy about this text. First, Gaius uses the same term (*potestas*) to describe the power over the slave as over the other members of the *familia* (hardly surprising as slaves were legally part of the *familia*). This most likely reflects the earliest position when the power over the family was undifferentiated and operated within the realm of the head of the household's domestic power. In second place, according to Gaius, the origin of this power is the *ius gentium*, a frequently used term in the works of the classical jurists. In its primary meaning, it referred to customs of the surrounding nations, a law of nations if you will. Notice also that Gaius focuses on two elements of the power which the master holds over the slave. On the one hand, the most savage of these rights (to destroy the slave), on the other a recognition that slaves could act on behalf of their owners, but not for themselves. We must assume that Gaius chose to highlight these two points with reason. On the one hand, the right over life and death was probably the most primitive element of the power which the master held, while on the other the use of the slave must have been a more recent development. To what extent the right of life and death was still available to the owner by the classical period is hard to tell. In all likelihood, Gaius is here discussing legal history.

It is a feature of classical Roman law that the position of the slave in relation to his owner is gradually improved through various legal measures which protect the slave from cruel treatment by his master. Take the following two comments:

> D. 48.8.11.2 (Modestinus, Rules, book 6). After the *Lex Petronia* [before 79 CE] and the Senatus Consulta relating to it, a master's power of consigning slaves to fight wild beasts on the basis of his

own [domestic] judgement was taken away. But if the master's complaint is a just one and the slave has been brought before a judge, this penalty can be inflicted. [translation: Handouts]

Inst.Gai.I.53. ... By constitution of the late Antonius [Pius] it is provided that anyone who kills his own slave without cause is as much subject to the law as one who kills someone else's. Even excessive severity on the part of the masters is restrained by a constitution of the same emperor; on being consulted by some provincial governors about slaves who take refuge at temples of the gods or the statutes of emperors, he ruled that masters whose harshness is found to be unbearable are to be forced to sell their slaves. [translation: Handouts]

One should not take these two texts to mean that all Romans treated their slaves cruelly as a matter of course. Slaves could be valuable financial commodities and it is unlikely that they would be destroyed or damaged by their owners at will. Nonetheless, laws are not made without good reason and it must be assumed that there is something behind these texts.

On the other side of the spectrum of statuses lay those people who had the full benefit of the Roman law of persons and family. Before 212 CE, access to Roman law was determined by Roman citizenship. There were a number of ways in which this could be acquired. The most common way was by birth from a valid Roman marriage (another through adoption). A birth of this kind automatically generated paternal authority, one of the cornerstones of the Roman law of persons and family. Gaius expresses it in the following manner:

Inst.Gai.I.55. Children whom we beget in civil marriages are also in our power. This right is peculiar to Roman citizens for scarcely any other men have over their sons a power such as we have. The divine Hadrian declared as much in a rescript he issued on these who petitioned him for citizenship for themselves and their children. I am not forgetting that the Galatians regard children as being in the power of their parents. [translation: Handouts]

In this text we see a report of the imperial bureaucracy in action. The Emperor Hadrian had been petitioned by some [unknown] individuals regarding citizenship. In response, he (no doubt on advice from his legal counsel) articulated the notion that paternal authority is peculiar to Roman citizens. In a patriarchal society such as Rome, children born in wedlock took the status of the father. This was important for the purposes of the law of succession where the principle of *agnatio* (blood relationship through the male ancestor) played an important role (illegitimate children did not inherit to the same extent as legitimate children).

The head of the household had extensive rights over his children (and grandchildren). Chief among these, by virtue of his parental power, was to accept the child into the family. According to various statutes from the reign of Augustus, children had to be registered (every male Roman citizen had three names to denote his family affiliation) within thirty days in order to confirm their legitimacy, and it has been suggested that birth registers were kept (Schulz, *Roman Law*, 75).

The only other ways to acquire Roman citizenship were through formal manumission from slavery or the granting of citizenship *en bloc* to an entire community as a reward for their allegiance to Rome. Gaius expresses it in the following way:

> Inst.Gai.I.11. The freeborn are those who are born free, freedmen are people who are manumitted from lawful slavery. Again, there are three classes of freedman: they are either Roman citizens or Latins or in the category of *dediticii* (those who have capitulated) [translation: Handouts]

As this text shows, prior to the enactment of the *Constitutio Antoniniana* of 212 CE, Roman law did not apply to all persons living within the boundaries of the Empire. The Empire consisted of Roman citizens with full rights and access to Roman private law as well as people of other 'statuses' such as *Latini* (persons who had been informally manumitted and therefore did not acquire citizenship), *dediticii* (those who had capitulated and who were prohibited by law from coming within 100 miles of the city of Rome) and peregrines (foreigners who may hold citizenship of other states or cities, but who were living in Roman territories). The effect of this decree was to remove the legal distinction between citizens and those with a lesser status.

The third important determinant of legal status was a person's place in the Roman family. The family in Roman law was an important legal entity, the prime purpose of which, from the perspective of the head of the household was twofold, namely to exercise authority over wives, children and slaves and to manage the assets of the family. It is important to stress that the Roman family was in no way similar to the modern concept of a 'nuclear family'. It was essentially a legal construct bound together by paternal authority and *agnatio*. Ulpian describes the family as follows:

D.50.16.195 (Ulpian, Edict, book 46). Let us see how the term 'family' (*familia*) is to be understood. It has indeed a variety of meanings: for it is applied both to things (*res*) and to persons. [translation: Handouts]

This text is revealing about Roman attitudes towards the family. It functioned as a smaller version of the Roman state and the legal importance of the family is clearly visible in a raft of legislation introduced by Augustus in an attempt to promote marriage as the only form of legitimate union among Romans. At the pinnacle of the Roman family was the head of the household, the oldest male of the family (usually the paternal grandfather). Roman law awarded the head of the household (*paterfamilias* in Latin) extensive rights over the persons and the property of the family. Ulpian describes it as follows:

D.1.6.4 (Ulpian, Institutes, book 1). A Roman citizen can be a *paterfamilias* or a son in power (*filius familias*) … or a daughter in power (*filia familias*). A *paterfamilias* is a man who has his own power (*potestas*), whether he is above or below the age of puberty … a son in power or a daughter in power is in the power of someone else. For a child born to the union between me and my wife is in my power; and one who is born from the union of my son and his wife, in other words my grandson or granddaughter is also in my power, as are my great-grandson or great-granddaughter and so on. [translation: Handouts]

These rights (collectively known as *patriapotestas*) were lifelong and only terminated by the death of the *paterfamilias* or the emancipation of the child. To modern eyes, many of these rights seem cruel and invasive (e.g. the right to expose infants and to interfere in relationships), but their existence should not necessarily be taken to imply that all heads of households ruled their families like small fiefdoms. It is more likely to be a reflection of the antiquity of this institution and its importance for the domestic jurisdiction of the head of the household over his family. See for example this description of the origins of paternal authority by the Greek scholar, Dionysius of Halicarnassus:

Romulus granted to the Roman father absolute power over his son, and this power was valid until the father's death, whether he decided to imprison him, or whip him, to put him in chains and make him work on a farm, or even to kill him. Romulus even allowed the

Roman father to sell his son into slavery. (Dionysius of Halicarnassus 2.26-7, taken from *FIRA* 1, p. 8) [translation: Sheldon §15]

Two aspects of this text are notable. First, paternal authority is connected to the founding father of Rome, thus reinforcing the idea of the antiquity of this institution. Secondly, the text only mentions 'sons'. This is deliberate as Dionysius is subtly reinforcing the point about *agnatio* through the male line. The text above by Ulpian does mention daughters though, although it makes one wonder whether this might be a later addition to the text.

In time, many aspects of the paternal authority were diluted. There is ample evidence that by the classical period some of these rights (e.g. the right to interfere in the relationships of his children and to insist on divorces) were being curtailed. See, for example, Ulpian's statement:

D.48.8.2 (Ulpian, Adulterers, book 1). A father cannot kill his son without a [public] hearing: he must bring criminal proceedings against him before the prefect or the provincial governor. [translation: Handouts]

We must not be too quick to use this as evidence of the curtailment of the father's power. Notice how the original context of the text referred to 'adulterers'. It may well be that this statement by Ulpian was made in relation to the penalties of the *Lex Iulia* on adultery which enabled the husband who caught his wife in the act of adultery in their home to slay the adulterer.

To understand the law relating to the Roman family, two aspects must be examined in greater detail, namely the relationships between husband and wife, and parent and child.

The main purpose of the Roman marriage was to create Roman citizens through birth, thereby to enlarge the family by way of *agnatio*.

Inst.Gai.I.156. Agnates (*agnati*) are those related to each other through people of the male sex, being as it were cognates (*cognati*) on the father's side, for instance your brother by the same father … or your paternal uncle …. Those connected through people of the female sex are not agnates, but cognates, related only by natural law. So between a mother's brothers and her son there is no *agnatio*, but there is *cognatio* … [translation: Handouts]

The distinction between *agnatio* and *cognatio* had an important impact on the Roman law of succession. We will return to this matter in Chapter 3. For a valid Roman marriage to take place, the parties had to be of marriageable age. In Roman law, this age was twelve for women and fourteen for men, ages agreed by the jurists as being the legal age of puberty. Although this seems quite young, it must be remembered that the average Roman life-expectancy was shorter than in modern times. Roman marriages were legally important for two reasons. First, any children born from such a marriage automatically obtained Roman citizenship by birth. In second place, children born from a valid marriage were subject to the *patriapotestas* of their head of the household.

A Roman marriage could be preceded by a betrothal. This typically occurred when the parties were not yet of a marriageable age. While in republican Roman law the betrothal could be formulated as a verbal contract, breach of which could lead to lawsuits, it had ceased to be actionable by the time of classical Roman law. This is indicative of a change in the understanding of marriage from a property transaction between two families to a social relationship between two individuals with the aim of producing Roman citizens.

In classical Roman law, the most common form of marriage was the 'free marriage' (marriage without *manus*). This term was used to distinguish it from the older form of marriage (marriage with *manus*) which still existed in classical Roman law, but which was entered into less frequently as it had a negative impact on the person and the property of the wife. Gaius describes the older regime in the following manner:

Inst.Gai.I.110. Once women passed in *manus* in three ways, by *usus*, by *confarreatio* and by *coemptio*. A woman passed into *manus* by *usus* if she lived continuously as a wife for one year, being as it were acquired by a year's prescription (*usucapio*) and so she passed into her husband's family ranking as a daughter. Thus it was laid down in the Twelve Tables that a woman not wishing to come under her husband's *manus* in this way should stay away from him for three nights each year (*trinoctium abesse*) and so interrupt the *usus* of that year. But all of this law has been partly abolished by statute and partly forgotten because of disuse. [translation: Handouts; *usucapio* is a form of prescriptive acquisition of title found in the law of property]

Although it is commonly said that there were no 'legal formalities' for a free marriage, this is not entirely accurate. It is fair to say that no ceremonies sanctioned by the state were required to create a free marriage (unlike the older form of marriage which required certain ceremonies to establish *manus*), but Roman law laid down certain requirements. The parties had to be of a marriageable age, unmarried and of the opposite sex. They had to have *conubium*, the capacity to marry as a component of their citizenship, and they had to fall outside the forbidden degrees of relationship.

> Inst.Gai.I.59. No marriage can be contracted and there is no *conubium* between persons standing in any relationship like parent and child to each other, for instance father and daughter ... grandfather and granddaughter ... [i.e. ascendants and descendants]. [translation: Handouts]

Free marriage in Roman law was based on consent of the parties (and of those in whose paternal power they stood). This is expressed by the jurist Paul in the following fashion:

> D.23.2.2 (Paul, Edict, book 35). A marriage cannot take place unless everyone involved consents, that is the parties and those in whose power they are.

Although in theory heads of household could interfere with their children's marriages by virtue of their paternal authority, there is evidence that this right was curtailed during the classical period:

> D.23.2.19 (Marcian, Institutes, book 16). By section 35 of the *Lex Iulia* [*de maritandis ordinibus* of 18 BCE] those who wrongfully prevent children (*liberos*) in their power from marrying or getting married (*ducere uxores vel nubere*) or who refuse to give them a dowry in accordance with the constitution of the divine Severus and Antoninus [*c.* 200 CE] can be compelled by the proconsuls or provincial governors to arrange marriages and provide dowries for them. Those who do not try to arrange marriages are held to prevent them. [translation: Handouts]

Notice that according to the final sentence of this text, sufferance is also deemed to be interference. It is important to note that Roman marriage was monogamous. Although sex outside marriage with the lower classes was not illegal (since people in this situation could not legally marry anyway), Augustus, through his legislation (principally the *Lex Iulia de Maritandis ordinibus* and the *Lex Iulia de Adulteriis*) attempted to regulate the private affairs of (presumably) the upper classes. The former act was designed to reinforce the institution of marriage by placing a legal duty on all citizens within a certain age range to marry and by penalising those who failed to do so, while the latter penalised sexual liaisons between those of the same class outside marriage by outlawing *stuprum* (free sexual intercourse with others of the same class outside marriage) and outlawed adultery. This law states:

> 'Henceforth no one shall commit adultery or rape knowingly or with malice aforethought' The words of this law apply both to him who abets and to him who commits the crime.

> The Julian law to control adultery punishes not only those who violate the marriages of others. Under the same law, the crime of debauchery [i.e. *stuprum*] is punished, when anyone seduces and violates, even without force, either a virgin or respectable widow. (*Acta Divi Augusti*, pp. 113-16, 123, 126) [translation: Shelton §77]

The legislation of Augustus introduced a legal duty on the husband to divorce the wife as soon as her adultery was discovered. The husband then had to prosecute his wife in the adultery courts created under this legislation. A successful prosecution led to loss of the dowry and even banishment. The two Julian acts were later supplemented by the *Lex Papia Poppaea* which imposed financial penalties on those who preferred to remain celibate or were childless. Whether these statutes achieved the desired result is difficult to assess, but authors of the period regarded them as unsuccessful. See, for example, the following comment by Tacitus:

> Towards the end of his life, Augustus passed the Papia-Poppaean Law, which supplemented the earlier Julian Laws, to encourage the enforcement of penalties for celibacy and to enrich the Treasury. However, even with this new law, marriages and births did not increase substantially. Childlessness offered too many advantages. (Tacitus, *Annals* 3.25) [translation: Shelton §40]

This rich passage contains a number of interesting points. Tacitus thought that the underlying motives for these acts were twofold, first to enrich the Treasury (i.e. financial) and secondly to increase the birth rate of Roman citizens (i.e. social). He seems ambivalent about the success of this legislation. While the former may have worked, the latter aim certainly was not fulfilled.

Exciting though this statement is, one should not take Tacitus' word as the gospel. Rather, it should be weighed up against other evidence to see how accurately it reflects the real position (as far as it can be ascertained).

Throughout the marriage, the parties had to manifest their intention to remain married (*affectio maritalis*) to the outside world by, for example, having a common marital home. Marriage contracts were not uncommon. Take the following example which, although Egyptian rather than Roman, would not have been incompatible with Roman law of the time:

> Thermion and Apollonius son of Ptolemaeus agree that they have come together for the purpose of sharing their lives with one another. The above-mentioned Apollonius son of Ptolemaeus agrees that he has received from Thermion, handed over from her household as a dowry, a pair of gold earrings [ ] From now on he will furnish Thermion, as his wedded wife, with all necessities and clothing according to his means, and he will not mistreat her or cast her out or insult her or bring in another wife; otherwise he will at once return the dowry and in addition half again as much. ... And Thermion will fulfil her duties toward her husband and her marriage and will not sleep away from the house or be absent one day without the consent of Apollonius son of Ptolemaeus and will not damage or injure their common home and will not consort with another man; otherwise she, if judged guilty of these actions, will be deprived of her dowry, and in addition the transgressor will be liable to the prescribed fine. ... (BGU 1052 (Selected Papyri, 3)) [translation: Shelton §57]

Notice the level of detail in this marriage contract. It seems not unlike a normal commercial partnership contract. Of particular interest are the rules concerning dowry and the return of the dowry as a penalty for transgressions within the marriage (such as adultery). One can clearly see from this contract how the dowry could be used as a measure to keep the parties together in marriage.

The free marriage, as a more liberal institution than its predecessor, did not affect the wife's existing property or place in the family. If she was under the paternal authority of her *paterfamilias* at the time of marriage, she remained as such until such time as the authority was terminated (usually through the death of the head of the household). She then became legally independent (*sui iuris*), but was subject to guardianship in relation to her commercial transactions. This is succinctly expressed by Ulpian in the following text:

> D.50.16.195 (Ulpian, Edict, book 46). A woman is both the first and
> last of her family. [translation: Handouts]

This text says much about the Roman legal attitude to women. Ulpian could not quite bring himself to state that a woman could be independent when she was in a free marriage and became *sui iuris* after her birth *paterfamilias* has died. He therefore had to invent a form of words that conveyed the idea that she was 'a family of one'. This statement demonstrates the importance of the *familia* as a legal concept in Roman law.

Given the separation of property between spouses which existed in classical Roman law, it comes as no surprise that gifts between spouses were not permitted. This ban was not aimed at small gifts, but rather at large commercial gifts which could potentially defraud creditors of one of the spouses. This can be seen from the following text:

> D.24.1.1 (Ulpian, Sabinus, book 32). It is an accepted custom with
> us that gifts between husband and wife are not valid. It is accepted
> in order to prevent people from impoverishing themselves through
> mutual affection by unreasonable gifts which are beyond their
> means. [translation: Handouts]

Notice how Ulpian mentions that it is a matter of 'accepted custom', in other words this rule of law has grown organically rather than being enacted by statute. Where such gifts had been made, they could be kept, but when the marriage ended in divorce the value of the gifts had to be returned. No doubt the intention with which it had been given would be key.

In a certain sense, the only exception to rule on gifts between spouses was the institution known as the dowry. The dowry was a fund of property or money given by the wife (if she was legally independent) or her family to the husband (such as the gold earrings in the marriage contract above). Ulpian tells us how a dowry is conventionally given:

> Ulpian, Regulae 6.3. Dowry is either called 'parental' (*profecticia*)
> when it is given by the wife's father, or 'external' (*adventicia*) when
> it is given by anyone else at all. [translation: Handouts]

Although the dowry became the property of the husband, there were various restrictions to his use of assets by the classical period. This development is linked to the rise of the free marriage, the ease of divorce and a change in the Roman conception of the purpose of a marriage. This is succinctly expressed by the jurist Tryphoninus:

D.23.3.75 (Tryphoninus, Disputations, book 6). Although the dowry is part of the husband's property, it nevertheless belongs to the wife [translation: Handouts]

Thus, the husband's ownership of the dowry was 'hollow', especially since the wife could compel its return in cases of divorce. Where a marriage failed through divorce, the husband normally had to return the dowry at once (or in instalments depending on the nature of the assets). In classical Roman law, certain automatic retentions were built into law which enabled the husband to retain part of the dowry. This can be seen from the following text:

Ulpian, Regulae 6.9. Retentions (*retentiones*) on the dowry can occur for children (*propter liberos*) for misconduct (*propter mores*) for expenses (*propter impensas*) for gifts (*propter res amotas*). 6.10 A retention for children can be made if the divorce was the fault (*culpa*) of the wife, or of her father where she is in power. Then a sixth of the dowry can be retained for each child, but not for more than three. [translation: Handouts]

Notice how this text by Ulpian assumes that the children will remain with the husband after the divorce (this also goes some way to explaining the position of the wife in the Roman law of succession, as we shall see in Chapter 3). Again, this reinforces the notion of parental authority coupled with *agnatio*.

Termination of the marriage occurred mainly in one of two ways, namely through death of one of the spouses or through divorce. Where the wife predeceased the husband, he could keep the dowry unless otherwise stipulated when it was granted to him. If the husband predeceased the wife, both she and the children would become legally independent (*sui iuris*) if the husband had also been the head of the household. The wife was placed under guardianship (only for the purposes of commercial transactions and litigation) and the children would be placed under tutorship depending on their age.

Divorce in classical Roman law could take place either through consent or by unilateral notification by one of the parties. Consensual divorce did not require any grounds, but frivolous divorces were discouraged by the fact that the dowry had to be returned either immediately or in instalments. Divorce by consent manifested itself in the cessation of the intention to remain married (*affectio maritalis*).

The sending of a unilateral notice of the intention to divorce seemingly required greater formality. The prescribed form of words seems to have been the following:

> D.24.2.2.1 (Gaius, Provincial Edicts, book 11). In repudiations, that is renunciation, these words are the approved ones: 'Keep your things to yourself!' or 'Look to your own things!' [translation: Handouts]

Certain texts suggest that the notice had to be sent in the presence of seven witnesses, but it is unclear whether this referred to all unilateral notices or merely those sent in compliance with the Augustan law on adultery. This is plausible, especially since the divorce in this case would not have been consensual. Take the following text:

> D.24.2.9 (Paul, Adultery, book 2). A divorce is invalid unless it takes place in the presence of seven Roman citizens of full age and also a freedman of the divorcing party.

A number of divorce agreements from Egypt display similarities with Roman law. Take the following example:

> Zois and Antipater agree that they have separated from one another and severed their arrangement to live together. ... And Zois agrees that Antipater has returned to her, handed over from his household, the items he received as her dowry, namely clothing valued at 120 silver drachmas and a pair of gold earrings. Both parties agree that henceforth the marriage contract will be null and void ... and from this day it will be lawful for Zois to marry another man and for Antipater to marry another woman, with neither party being liable to prosecution. (BGU 1103 (Selected Papyri, 6)) [translation: Shelton §71]

This appears to be a divorce by consent and the parties agree to sever their *affectio maritalis* by ceasing to live together. Furthermore, an arrangement for the return of the dowry is made. Finally, the parties take care to state that the marriage is now null and void so that they are free to marry others without falling foul of the law on adultery.

Before moving on to the relationship between parent and child, a few observations about the legal position of Roman women are required. Roman women had extensive rights under private law compared to other societies of the period, but they were entirely debarred from public law.

This meant that they could not vote or hold public office, nor could they act as witnesses or legal representatives in a court of law. This attitude towards women is not incompatible with the patriarchal structure of Roman society, but in matters of private law their position was much better than that of their Greek counterparts. Women who became *sui iuris* owing to the death of the *paterfamilias* were under perpetual guardianship (for certain aspects of their life).

> Guardians are appointed both for males and females; for males only when they have not yet reached puberty and are therefore of tender age; or females both before and after puberty because they are the weaker sex and are ignorant in business and legal matters ...
>
> A woman needs authority from her guardian in the following matters: if she is engaging in a lawsuit, if she is undertaking a legal or financial obligation, if she is transacting in civil business (Ulpian, *Regulae* 11.1, 21, 27, 28) [translation: Shelton §50]

The guardian could be appointed by will (usual practice) or in some cases a woman could also choose her own guardian. The guardian had a limited function. He could not undertake any transactions with her property, but merely had a right to veto transactions of which he did not approve. He could not be sued as a guarantor for any debts incurred by her. There is a relaxation of the rules on guardianship for women during the classical period.

The legal relationship between parent and child is based on two principles, namely paternal power and *agnatio*. It has been pointed out that many of the topics with which this area of law concerns itself in modern law such as parental responsibilities and matters of custody in the event of divorce did not surface in Roman law. Owing to the concept of paternal power (*patriapotestas*) which the father (if head of the household) exerted over his children, issues of custody were immaterial as the children, in the event of divorce, always stayed with the father. As mentioned above, paternal power was created by birth out of a valid Roman marriage (or through adoption) and existed until terminated either by the death of the head of the household or, artificially, through emancipation. This is expressed by Gaius as follows:

> Inst.Gai.I.132. Children cease to be in parental power by emancipation. [translation: Handouts]

By virtue of this power, the father (if head of the household) acquired extensive power over the person and property of his children. As far as his rights over the person of his children were concerned, many parallels have been drawn with the position of the slave in the household. One can see this from Gaius' analogy in the following text:

Inst.Gai.II.87. Anything received by children in our *potestas* or our slaves, whether by conveyance (*mancipatio*) or delivery, or under a verbal contract (*stipulatio*) or on any other basis is acquired for us, because a person in our *potestas* can have nothing of his own. [translation: Handouts]

The most intrusive of these rights permitted the head of the household to expose newborn infants (a right abolished during the latter part of the fourth century CE) and the right to interfere in the relationships of his children by forbidding marriage or insisting on a divorce (though as we have seen these rights were curtailed during the classical period). As far as the property of the children is concerned, early Roman law held that children could not own any property separately from the head of the household. By the classical period, this position had been severely undermined by permitting children to hold a *peculium*, a fund similar to those held by slaves, over which they had some rights even though technically it remained the property of the *paterfamilias*.

D.14.6.2 (Ulpian, Edict, book 46). As far as the military *peculium* is concerned, a *filius familias* is in just the same position as if he were a *paterfamilias*. [translation: Handouts]

Various further improvements were made during the course of the classical period whereby other categories of good were also brought within the ambit of the child's *peculium*, such as goods specifically inherited from their mother.

Paternal authority was lifelong and could only be terminated in one of two ways, namely either through the death of the head of the household or through the emancipation of the child. If, through the death of the head of the household, children became legally independent, Roman law stated that their interests had to be protected by tutors or guardians. If the child was an infant (i.e. below the age of seven) or an *impubes* (above the age of seven, but below the age of puberty), they were assigned a tutor. The tutor was responsible for the financial welfare of the child and had to authorise their transactions. Classical Roman law witnessed an evolution in the protection measures available to the child against a tutor. Above the age of puberty, children who were legally independent were placed under guardianship until they reached majority (at the age of twenty-five). The rules on guardianship are detailed and are best left for a more comprehensive treatment in another book.

A final aspect of the law of persons which requires mention is that of adoption. In Roman law, adoption could take one of two forms: the adoption of a person under paternal power (*alieni iuris*) or the adoption (properly called *adrogatio*) of one who is already *sui iuris*. In both cases, the motivation for adoption seems to have been the continuation of the Roman *familia* and the creation of an heir for the purposes of inheritance. The main consequence of adoption was that the adoptee became part of the *familia* and that the head of the household asserted paternal authority over him. The Roman legal rules on adoption (and especially on *adrogatio*) are detailed and best viewed within the larger context of the purpose of this institution.

Suggested further reading

Bradley, K. *Discovering the Roman Family* (Oxford 1991)

Dixon, S. *The Roman Family* (Baltimore, MD 1992)

Evans-Grubbs, J. *Women and the Law in the Roman Empire: A Sourcebook on Marriage, Divorce and Widowhood* (London 2002)

Gardner, J. *Family and Familia in Roman Law and Life* (Oxford 1998)

Saller, R. *Patriarchy, Property and Death in the Roman Family* (Cambridge 1994)

Treggiari, S. *Roman Marriage: iusti coniuges from the Time of Cicero to the Time of Ulpian* (Oxford 1993)

Chapter 3
'Things'

The second branch of the threefold division of all of private law which Gaius employs in his Institutes is that of the law of 'things'. He explains it as follows:

> Inst.Gai.II.1 In the previous book we dealt with the law of persons. Now we turn to things [*res*]. [translation: Handouts]

The inspiration for this threefold classification need not detain us here, but it most likely had its origins in philosophy. Suffice it to say that Gaius was not the first jurist to attempt to structure a branch of Roman private law. Attempts of this kind had already been made during the course of the late Republic, such as when the jurist Quintus Mucius Scaevola published a book in which he attempted to structure the law. Structure is important as it allows us to see logical connections between different areas of the law. It must be borne in mind, however, that our modern understanding of structure and categories is not necessarily that of the Romans. The Roman jurists had a very particular way of looking at structure, categories and definitions which was largely drawn from their education in Greek philosophy and the logic which drove it. Thus, although we might be tempted to reduce these Roman legal structures and categories to fit our modern understanding of structure and categories, this would be to project our own experiences onto the past without allowing it to speak for itself.

The law of 'things' consisted of three definite sub-categories. In modern law, these would be termed the law of property, the law of obligations and the law of succession. To the Roman legal mind, these three branches of law were conceptually united by their involvement with 'things'. Again, even in this threefold subdivision of the law of 'things', the person-centred nature of Roman law is visible. The first branch deals with 'my things', the second with the interaction between 'my things' and those of others. The third branch of law deals with the distribution of 'my things' when I am no longer here. From this we can see that the individual, as we have seen in the previous chapter, is an important agent in Roman law.

3.1. Property

Traditionally, most textbooks on the subject start with the divisions of property found in Roman legal texts (chiefly in the Institutes of Gaius) since categorisation was the logical starting point in the Roman legal mind for any discussion of property. Let Gaius be our guide:

> Inst.Gai.II.1. … Now we turn to things. They are either regarded as private property (*in patrimonio*) or outside the sphere of private property (*extra patrimonium*).

> Inst.Gai.II.2. The primary division is twofold: things are subject to religious law (*divini iuris*) or secular law (*humani iuris*) … 3 Sacred things (*res sacrae*) are those consecrated to the gods above, religious things (*res religiosae*) are dedicated to the spirits of the dead (*Manes*), … 6 We can choose to make our own land religious by burying a corpse there, provided the deceased's funeral is our business. … 8 Again sanctified things (*res sanctae*) like walls and gates are in a sense subject to religious law. 9 A thing subject to religious law belongs to nobody (*nullius in bonis*), whereas something subject to secular law often belongs to someone, though it may belong to nobody …. 10 Things subject to secular law are either public or private. 11 Public things are held to belong to nobody as they are the property of the community (*res universitatis*). Private things belong to individuals.

> Inst.Gai.II.14a. There is another division of things: some are *mancipi* and others are *nec mancipi*. *Res mancipi* are land and houses on Italian soil: Slaves; animals normally trained to pull or carry things like oxen, horses, mules and asses and also rustic praedial servitudes. Urban praedial servitudes are *res nec mancipi*. 15 Stipendiary and tributary lands [i.e. provincial land] are not capable of mancipation. [translation: Handouts]

Notice that there are at least three types of division employed in this these texts: (1) private property/not private property; (2) subject to human law/subject to divine law; (3) *res mancipi* and *res nec mancipi*. While there is a tendency in the modern mind to try to fit these schemes together, this should be avoided as the Romans did not think in this manner. Rather, these should be seen as alternative modes of classifying property with a view to establishing one larger point, namely that certain types of 'things' fell outside the ambit of the law of property on account of their nature. Or, to phrase it differently, certain things could not be owned by individuals. Using this as our starting point, we can see that Gaius wished to stress that the law of property only really applied to those things subject to secular law and which were private in the sense that they could be privately owned. Within this category it was possible to use an earlier mode of classification (*res mancipi/res nec mancipi*) which had its origins in ancient Roman law.

What was the motivation for this distinction? The significance lay in its effect on the transfer of ownership. Gaius explains it as follows:

Inst.Gai.II.18. Now there is an important difference between *res mancipi* and *res nec mancipi* 19 *Res nec mancipi* become fully the property of someone else (*pleno iure*) by delivery alone, as long as they are corporeal and so can be delivered. 29 So if I deliver clothes or gold or silver to you, whether because of a sale or gift or on any other basis, it becomes yours immediately, as long as I am its owner. … 22 *Res mancipi* on the other hand are transferred to someone else by *mancipatio*; that is why they are called *res mancipi*. But *in iure cessio* works as well as *mancipatio*. [translation: Handouts]

In this text, Gaius explains one of the most fundamental concepts of the law of property. The Romans (as in modern civil-law systems) distinguished between cause and conveyance. The cause referred to the legally valid reason why ownership was transferred from one party to another and the conveyance referred to the ritual act which facilitated the transfer of ownership. So, in the cases mentioned above by Gaius, the cause would have been the sale or the gift, the conveyance would be the act (delivery or *mancipatio*).

For *res mancipi*, a formal ceremony was required whereas the same level of formality was not required for *res nec mancipi*. Gaius describes the *mancipatio* procedure in the following terms:

Inst.Gai.I.119. *Mancipatio* as we have already said, is a kind of symbolic sale (*imaginaria venditio*) and it too is an institution peculiar to Roman citizens. This is how it is done. In the presence of not less than five Roman citizens above the age of puberty as witnesses and a sixth person with the same qualification to hold the bronze scales, called a scale-holder (*libripens*), the person who is taking by the conveyance (*mancipium*) holds the property [or the bronze] and says: 'I declare that this slave is mine by the Quiritary law (*ex iure Quiritium*) and let him have been bought by me [or and he has been bought by me] (*emptus esto* or *est*) with this bronze and bronze scales. Then he strikes the scales with the bronze and gives it to the person from whom he is receiving by the conveyance as if it were the price (*quasi pretii loco*). [translation: Handouts]

The ritual described here suggests a procedure of considerable antiquity. It does not take much to appreciate that this formal requirement was not particularly conducive to the demands of commerce. Also, given the large number of foreigners who did not have access to Roman civil law and the increase in the number of things which were not *res mancipi* and yet formed part of commercial transactions, it comes as little surprise that this category and the mode of conveyance associated with it was in decline during the classical period. Although it continued to exert some influence on the transfer of ownership of certain types of property, in practice the modes of conveyance of ownership which required less formality such as delivery (*traditio*) must have become more common. Take, for example, the following text:

Inst.Gai.II.65. It appears from what we have said that some things become the property of someone else (*alienari*) by natural law, as where they are transferred by delivery (*traditio*), and some by civil law; for *mancipatio*, *in iure cessio* and *usucapio* are confined to Roman citizens. [translation: Handouts]

Gaius' point in this text is that the older forms of conveyance such as *mancipatio* (and also *cessio in iure*) were peculiar to Roman citizens, while the modes that required less formality like delivery (*traditio*) arose out of the law of nature. By referring to the law of nature, Gaius is reinforcing the point that these modes are derived from external influences (natural law). We shall return to these modes of acquisition of ownership presently. For the moment is sufficient to note that *traditio* must have been the most common form of conveyance during the classical period.

Owing to the fact that prior to 212 CE Roman law applied only to Roman citizens (or those foreigners who had been granted the privilege of engaging in commerce with the Romans using their own law, said privilege being called the *ius commercii*), it is not possible to speak of one unified idea of 'ownership' in Roman law for much of the classical period. Since the focus of Gaius' textbook is Roman law as it applies to Roman citizens, it comes as little surprise that the 'form' of ownership on which he focuses most of his attention is ownership according to Roman law. The term used is *dominium ex iure quiritium*. This phrase, which the

Romans never define (nor did they need to as definitions were not really central to Roman legal thought), is pregnant with meaning. Let us take the first word, *dominium* – a word which is etymologically related to *dominus* (boss, lord). By describing someone as having *dominium* of an object, you are implying that they are the boss of it and that they have the strongest entitlement to the property. Such an entitlement can only arise out of a legally valid reason supplemented by an appropriate mode of conveyance. The second phrase is also quite telling. By linking the idea of ownership to the *Quirites* (a term which appears frequently in Virgil's *Aeneid* and which links Roman civilisation with Aeneas and the Trojans) the Roman jurists reinforced the point that Roman ownership was a uniquely Roman and hallowed entitlement to objects which was as old as their civilisation itself.

The pluralist nature of ownership in Roman law prior to 212 CE is nowhere more clearly visible than in the concepts of 'provincial' and 'peregrine' ownership. Ownership (in the sense of *dominium ex iure quiritium*) could only be held over Italic land (or land which had been given the privilege of 'Italic soil') by Roman citizens. Land in the provinces was incapable of private ownership as it was deemed to be *res publica*, i.e. belonging to the Roman state. The only type of right at private law which could be acquired over such land was a form of protected possession (*uti frui habere possidere*) subject to the payment of an annual tribute (Kaser/Knûtel §22.10). In the time of Gaius, there were two types of provincial land: stipendiary land was located in provinces 'belonging' to the Roman people (but administered by the senate) and tributary land was located in provinces 'belonging' to the emperor. In both cases, those who lived on such lands had to pay taxes (*stipendium/tributum*). Since these lands were *res nec mancipi*, 'ownership' could be transferred through a delivery alone. This may explain the legal context of the following text from Roman Britain (an imperial province):

> … Whereas, on arriving at the property in question, the wood Verlucionium, fifteen *arepennia* more or less, which is in the canton of the Cantiaci in Dibussu [ ] parish, [ ] neighboured by the heirs [of …] and the heirs of Caesennius Vitalis and the vicinal road, Lucius Junius Bellicus said that he had bought it from Titius Valerius Silvinus for forty denarii, as is contained in the deed of purchase … [On this tablet, see R.S.O. Tomlin, 'A five-acre wood in Roman Kent' in *Interpreting Roman London: Papers in Memory of Hugh Chapman* ed. J. Bird et al., 209-15 (Oxford 1996).] [translation: Tomlin 211]

As with so many documents of this kind, the text breaks off at a crucial point. What we can deduce from it, though, is that two Roman citizens (we assume their names were given) transacted for the sale of a wood and that the sale was recorded in writing. It being provincial land, the purchaser would not have acquired *dominium* in the strict sense by virtue of the conveyance (delivery), merely some form of possession which was protected at law. He would still have to pay an annual tribute to the imperial treasury.

The position of foreigners must also be borne in mind. Some legal texts refer to 'peregrine ownership', that is, 'ownership' held by foreigners living in Roman territories according to their own laws. Unfortunately, given the focus of Gaius' Institutes, too little information remains to speculate about the nature of this concept and how it interacted with Roman ownership. One thing is certain: the promulgation in 212 CE of the *Constitutio Antoniniana* which granted Roman citizenship to most of the free inhabitants of the Roman Empire must have had a significant impact on the plurality of 'ownership' in Roman law (especially in Egypt). The effect of this enactment seems to have been twofold. First, it demolished the distinction between Roman and peregrine ownership, since most free people within the boundaries of the Roman Empire now had Roman citizenship. Secondly, it must have undermined the distinction between Roman ownership of Italic land and Roman 'ownership' of provincial land. This may be one of the reasons why Diocletian abolished the distinction in the early fourth century CE.

Apart from ownership, the most complete entitlement which a person could exert over property, the Roman jurists also developed a number of more limited entitlements which persons could exercise over the property of others. This development was no doubt a product of the increasing sophistication of property law. These rights were not as comprehensive as ownership, but entitled the holder to some level of legal protection. The oldest category of these (what we would call limited real rights in modern law) arose out of agricultural practice where the grid-like system of Roman surveying caused some plots of land to be cut off from water sources or main roads. Thus, a legal institution had to be created to allow the owners of such land to have access to such resources, which may be located on the land of another, and to regulate the relationship between the owner of that land and the other party. Gaius describes it as follows:

Inst.Gai.IV.3. An action *in rem* is one in which we claim either that some corporeal thing is ours, or that we are entitled to some right such as use (*usus*) or usufruct (*utendi fruendi*), a right of way on foot (*iter*), a right to drive across (*actus*) a right to channel water (*acquaeductus*), a right to raise a building (*altius tollendi*) or prospect (*prospiciendi*). On the other hand, an action to deny these (*negativa*) is open to our opponent. [translation: Handouts]

Notice how Gaius speaks of an *actio in rem* (we will return to this concept in greater detail in our discussion of the law of procedure in Chapter 4). One could use this action to claim that one had 'some right' over the property of another. He then lists some of the more ancient ones which applied mostly to property situation in a rural location. These rights were collectively called servitudes and they were deemed to be (in theory) perpetual and attached to the land. Since they imposed a burden on someone else's property, they could only be created in a formal manner. Take the following statement by Julian:

D.8.2.34 (Julian, Minicius, book 2). A man who has two tracts of vacant ground can, on the conveyance of one of them, impose a servitude in favour of the other. [translation: Handouts]

Here, the creation of the servitude is linked to the formal conveyance of the land which, assuming it was Italic land, had to be done using a *mancipatio*. Since provincial land could not be owned in this way, the Romans had to devise specific rules for the creation of servitudes on provincial land. Gaius tells us the following:

Inst.Gai.II.31. ... If on the other hand it is over provincial lands that a man wishes to create a usufruct or right of way [etc.] ... he can do this only by means of pacts and stipulations, because these lands are not susceptible of either *mancipatio* or *in iure cessio*. [translation: Handouts]

Because the existence of servitudes created a relatively complex relationship between the owner of the property and the other party, Roman law developed sophisticated rules to minimise conflict. Take the following example:

D.8.1.9 (Celsus, Digest, book 5). Suppose a man is granted or bequeathed a right of way (*via*) without reservation over another's estate. He may walk and drive across it without restriction, that is across any part he chooses, as long as he does it in a reasonable way (*civiliter modo*): a general mode of expression is always subject to a tacit reservation. He need not be allowed to walk through the homestead (*villa*) itself, or among the vineyards, if he could have gone another way with less damage to the servient estate. Indeed it is settled he ought to walk or drive only along the route decided at the start .... [translation: Handouts]

Notice how in this text the criterion 'reasonable manner' is used to assess the conduct of the holder of the usufruct.

The oldest category of servitudes, which date back to the time of the Twelve Tables, were those which attached themselves to land. In time, this category was supplemented by another, collectively known as personal servitudes. They are described in the Digest as follows:

D.8.1.1 (Marcian, Rules, book 3). Servitudes are either attached to persons, like use (*usus*) and usufruct (*usufructus*) or to property as in the case of servitudes of rustic and urban estates. [translation: Handouts]

The main difference between these two categories was that personal servitudes did not attach themselves to the land. They were created for the benefit of a specific person (such as a widow or a ward) and thus only endured as long as the named beneficiary was alive (this was an offshoot of the Roman concept of universal succession upon inheritance, as we shall presently see):

D.7.4.3.3. (Ulpian, Sabinus, book 17). That a usufruct is also lost by death does not admit of any doubt, since the right of enjoyment is extinguished by death, just like any other right which attaches to the person. [translation: Handouts]

They could also be extinguished by non-use for a period of time. Like real servitudes, personal servitudes also had an impact on the owner's use of the property. In a sense they were more invasive as they enabled the holder to use and draw the fruits of the property without burdening them with responsibilities of ownership. To regulate the relationship between these competing interests, the Roman jurists developed the following principle:

D.7.1.1 (Paul, Vitellius, book 3). Usufruct is the right to use and enjoy (*ius utendi fruendi*) the things of another without impairing their substance (*salva rerum substantia*). [translation: Handouts]

Depending on the nature of the property, the holder of the usufruct had to ensure that his exploiting of the property did not have a negative impact on its 'substance', a philosophical idea which referred to the essence of the property. The Roman jurists discussed this aspect in great detail. As for the exploitation of the property, this could sometimes create complex legal problems. Take, for example, the following case:

> Inst.Gai.II.91. With regard to slaves over whom we have a usufruct, the rule is that whatever they acquire in connection with out affairs or from their own work is acquired for us, but that anything they acquire outside these two accounts belongs to the owner whose property they are. [translation: Handouts]

In this case, one person owned the slave while another held a usufruct over him. Gaius explains that the capacity of the slave to make money is divided between the holder of the usufruct and the owner of the slave.

One other form of 'limited real right' which requires mention is that of real security. It was a peculiar area of the law of property as it straddled both property and contract (the common way in which real securities were created.) Real security referred to the scenario where the financial value of objects was used to raise capital. Thus, where someone owned a valuable statue and needed to raise a loan, they went to a money-lender who lent them money against the value of the statue. By law, the money-lender acquired a real right over the statue. Under Roman law, two forms of real security were available. The more antiquated form involved the handing over of the statue to the money-lender for the duration of the loan, while the more developed form did not require the relinquishing of such possession. Should the debtor fail to repay the loan according to the terms agreed, the money-lender, by virtue of his rights in real security, acquired the right to attach and even sell the object to recover the loan. We will discuss this further in our treatment of the law of contracts.

The formalities attached to certain modes of conveyance in Roman law, coupled with the complexities surrounding the 'ownership' of provincial land, necessitated the existence of a flexible concept which could protect those who had a legitimate interest in property, but who did not necessarily have ownership. Gaius describes it as follows:

> Inst.Gai.II.40. ... in olden times ... a man was either Quiritary owner or he was not considered owner at all. But later ownership became divisible, so that one man may be Quiritary owner, and another 'bonitary owner' (*in bonis habere*). 41 So if I neither mancipate nor

cede *in iure* a *res mancipi* to you, but just deliver it, you become
bonitary owner, but I will still be Quiritary owner, until you have
usucaped it by possession. Once *usucapio* is complete, it becomes
fully yours .... [translation: Handouts]

The scenario described by Gaius in this passage is one of the main reasons
for the rise of possession. In this case, the parties had intended to transfer
ownership, but for some reason had used an inappropriate mode of
conveyance. This meant that ownership did not transfer and that the
person who had acquired the property did not become the owner as
intended. To protect him from external claims, Roman law developed the
idea of 'bonitary ownership' (a form of protected possession) until such
time as his entitlement to the property could mature into full ownership
through the passage of time.

Possession denoted physical control of a piece of property coupled
with a certain mental intention (either to be the owner as in the example
above or to exercise a legitimate entitlement over the property by virtue
of, say, another right). Unlike ownership, which was classified as the most
complete entitlement to property, possession was a question of fact which
depended on the continued physical control of the property (not just
personally, but also via other persons such as slaves and dependant
children). This may account for this celebrated statement by Ulpian:

D.41.2.12.1 (Ulpian, Edict, book 70). Ownership has nothing in
common with possession: so someone who has raised a *vindicatio*
over some property is not to be denied the interdict *uti possidetis*.
He is not held to have renounced possession by bringing a *vindicatio*. [translation: Handouts; *vindicatio* is the action to claim ownership; the *interdictum uti possidetis*, a Praetorian Interdict designed
to protect existing possession]

Certain forms of possession (on account of the reason why a person had
acquired possession in the first place) were protected in Roman law by
remedies granted by the praetor. Gaius tells us the following:

Inst.Gai.IV.139. In certain cases the praetor ... interposes his authority
in order to end disputes. He does this mainly when the parties are
contending over possession or quasi-possession. Basically he orders
or forbids something being done. The *formulae* or pleadings used for
this are called interdicts (*interdicta*). [translation: Handouts]

Inst.Gai.IV.148. An interdict for retaining possession is usually issued when two parties are disputing as to the ownership of some property, and the preliminary question of which of the litigants is to be in possession and which is to be pursuer arises. This is why the interdicts *uti possidetis* and *utrubi* have been provided. 149 The interdict *uti possidetis* is given in respect of the possession of land or houses, the interdict *utrubi* in respect of the possession of movables. [translation: Handouts]

D.43.17.1pr (Ulpian, Edict, book 69). The praetor says 'I forbid the use of force to prevent whichever of you now possesses this building (the subject of the action) without force, stealth or licence as against the other party (*nec vi nec clam nec precario ab altero*) from continuing so to possess it.' [translation: Handouts]

These were summary remedies designed to preserve the status quo until such time as the issue of ownership could be resolved. It has often been asked why Roman law chose to protect possession, sometimes even at the expense of ownership. Various justifications have been offered, namely that it prevents violence and that it encourages the resolution of disputes. In reality, the reasons for the rise of possession are probably many and varied and include both the ones mentioned here as well as those mentioned above.

Having explored these two central concepts, we must now turn to ways in which one could acquire ownership in property. As mentioned above, one of the central purposes of the different modes of classification of property in Roman law was to highlight the fact that different types of property required different modes of conveyance. Roman legal texts contain much discussion on the different modes of acquiring ownership. The significance of these modes is twofold. First, they are broadly grouped into two categories (civil-law modes and natural-law modes). Gaius tells us the following:

Inst.Gai.II.65. It appears from what we have said that some things become the property of someone else (*alienari*) by natural law, as where they are transferred by delivery (*traditio*), and some by civil law; for *mancipatio, in iure cessio* and *usucapio* are confined to Roman citizens.

The reference to natural law here is important. As mentioned before, Gaius uses it here mainly to reinforce the point that the civil-law modes are peculiarly Roman (and therefore could only be used by Roman citizens prior to 212 CE), while the natural-law modes were more broadly available to everyone regardless of their status.

Of the civil-law modes, the most important were *mancipatio, cessio in iure* and *usucapio*. The former two were already of some antiquity by the advent of the classical period and describe the earliest modes of transfer of ownership. As we have seen above from a description of the act, *mancipatio* was a ritual that involved witnesses and a symbolic 'sale' of the object present, while *cessio in iure* required the presence of a magistrate to transfer ownership of property. The latter was even more cumbersome than the former, as we can see from this comment by Gaius:

> Inst.Gai.II.25. Usually, however, indeed nearly always, we use *mancipatio* because there is no need for us to do with greater difficulty before a praetor or provincial governor what we can do for ourselves in the presence of friends. [translation: Handouts]

Nonetheless, it was required for certain types of conveyance on account of the nature of the object:

> Inst.Gai.II.29. While urban praedial servitudes can only be ceded *in iure* rustic ones can also be mancipated. 30 Usufruct can only be ceded *in iure* … . [translation: Handouts]

Usucapio was a mode of acquisition which rectified some of the problems inherent in insisting on a very formal mode of acquisition of ownership. Through the passage of time and under certain conditions, defects in the transfer of ownership could be 'cured', resulting in full *dominium* (we have already encountered this above in relation to bonitary ownership).

> Inst.Gai.II.41. So if I do not mancipate or surrender *in iure* as *res mancipi* to you, but just deliver it, it becomes yours *in bonis* but remains mine by Quiritary right until you have usucaped it by possession. Once *usucapio* is complete you are fully entitled (*pleno iure*) to it, both *in bonis* and by Quiritary right, just as if it had been mancipated or surrended *in iure*. [translation: Handouts]

In classical Roman law, the fact of possession was further refined into a number of additional requirements, namely that the holder had to have acquired it in good faith, pursuant to a lawful cause and that the object had not been stolen. All of these should be seen as ways in which to further circumscribe the conditions under which this institution could operate.

Usucapio was an institution of some antiquity which was already prevalent at the time of the Twelve Tables, as Gaius tells us:

> Inst.Gai.II.42. *Usucapio* of movables is completed in one year, that of lands and buildings in two. This is laid down by the Twelve Tables. [translation: Handouts]

> Inst.Gai.II.44. This system appears to have been adopted to prevent there being uncertainty over the ownership of property for too long. The periods of one or two years required for *usucapio* by a possessor are sufficient for an owner to trace his property. [translation: Handouts]

The natural-law modes, so called because they were not unique to Roman law, form a disparate category which covers a wide range of circumstances. They include matters such as the capture of ownerless property, the creation of a new object out of raw materials belonging to different owners and the finding of treasure on another's land. Let us look at a few examples:

> Inst.Gai.II.66. It is not just those things we acquire by delivery which become ours by natural reason, but also those we acquire by occupation (*occupatio*), because they did not previously belong to anyone (*res nullius*) for example every creature captured on land, in the sea or in the air. [translation: Handouts]

> D. 41.1.26pr (Paul, Sabinus, book 14). ... Proculus declares that the rule in force is that which has been approved by Servius and Labeo. In the case of objects which have a proper quality (*propria qualitas*), anything added to them is merged with the whole; for instance, a foot or hand with a statue, the bottom or handle with a cup, a bed-post with a bed, a board with a ship. The whole statue, cup, bed, ship or building still belongs to its former owner. [translation: Handouts]

The principle expressed in the first text is that of 'first capture of ownerless property'. By seizing something which is without owner, the property becomes ours through the exercise of our right to seizure. It does not take much to appreciate that such a mode would have been a very useful *ex post facto* intellectual justification to a conquering civilisation such as the

Romans. What Gaius is articulating in this text is merely a legal justification for a very ancient notion, namely 'first come, first served'. The second
text articulates a more complicated notion which in legal terms is called
accessio or merger. If two objects belonging to different owners are
merged inseparably into one, who becomes the owner of the composite
(especially where this has been done without consent)? Notice how, in
the examples given here, it is possible to identify a primary object (the
armless statue) and a secondary object (the arm) – this was an important
notion in determining who had ownership of the newly created thing. The
rule articulated in this text is that the owner of the primary object also
becomes the owner of the secondary object through the act of merger. Of
course, depending on the intention with which the separation had been
done and by whom, the owner of the secondary object (the arm) could be
expected to be compensated. Given the theoretical and logical puzzles
thrown up by these modes, they provided much room for juristic discussion, but one cannot help but think that much of these discussions are
theoretical/didactic rather than actual legal queries.

Arguably the most important (and practically useful) example of a
natural-law mode was that of delivery. It was the standard way of
transferring ownership of anything which was not *res mancipi* and its lack
of formality contributed to its increasing popularity as a mode of transferring ownership. Take this statement by Gaius:

> Inst.Gai.II.19. For *res nec mancipi* became wholly another's prop-
> erty by delivery (*traditio*) alone, provided they are corporeal and so
> can be delivered. 21 The same applies to provincial lands ….
> [translation: Handouts]

Given the lack of formality attached to this mode of conveyance, it does
not take much to appreciate that it would have been very useful in practice.
The final comment regarding provincial land is particularly telling. If all
provincial land (prior to 212 CE) could not be 'owned' according to
Roman civil law, the only way to obtain a valid conveyance in order to
become the 'provincial owner' of a piece of land was by way of *traditio*
pursuant to a cause such as sale or donation. This can be seen from the
following text:

> D.41.1.31pr (Paul, Edict, book 31). Mere delivery (*nuda traditio*)
> never transfers ownership, but only if it is preceded by a sale or some
> other just cause (*iusta causa*) for delivery. [translation: Handouts]

But how could one convey ownership of land if for delivery to take place there had to be a 'handing over' of the property? To increase the utility of this mode, the Roman jurists devised analogous modes to take account of the different types of property. Take the following example:

> D. 41.2.1.21 (Paul, Edict, book 54). … That it is unnecessary to take possession by physical contact (*corpore et tactu*) but that it can be done by sight and intention (*oculis et affectu*) is proved [Priscus] says, by those things which owing to their great weight cannot be moved such as columns. For these are considered to be delivered if the parties consent in the presence of the thing …. [translation: Handouts]

It is interesting to note that there are no corresponding discussions in Roman legal texts concerning the modes of acquisition of possession. In fact, other than some mention of the different types of possession and how these were protected, there is little else to be gleaned from the texts. Why is this? The obvious answer lies in the difference between ownership and possession. Ownership was the highest legal entitlement to property which could only be acquired through certain well-established modes of conveyance whereas possession was merely a state of fact which required legal protection under certain circumstances.

The main remedy for the asserting of ownership was the *vindicatio rei*. It was a legal action only available to the owner of the property under Roman law. It is a remedy which developed during the Republic and allowed the owner of the property to reclaim it from any third party by asserting his ownership over the property. Ulpian tells us the following about the remedy:

> D.6.1.1 (Ulpian, Edict, book 16). Such an action *in rem* to recover a specific thing (*specialis*) is available for all moveable property, animate and inanimate, and also where land is involved. [translation: Handouts]

Notice the wide scope which this action had, the only restriction being that it could only be brought in respect of corporeal property. As we will see in chapter 4, the 'action' mentioned here was based on a specialist 'formula' which dictated to the parties which words they had to use to frame their lawsuit. For the *vindicatio* the *formula* consisted of statements such as:

Inst.Gai.IV.41 The *intentio* is the part of the *formula* in which the pursuer states his claim, for example … 'if it appears that the slave belongs to Aulus Agerius by Quiritary rights' [Aulus Agerius being the stock name given to the plaintiff]. [translation: Handouts]

Notice that the *formula* states 'if it appears …'. This means that the person asserting ownership of the slave has to bring evidence that he owns it by Quiritary right, in other words that they have *dominium ex iure quiritium*. How could one prove this? The easiest way would be to demonstrate that you had acquired the property on the grounds of a legally justifiable reason (the *causa*), for example that it was sold to you by the rightful owner and that you had paid for it, and secondly that an appropriate mode of conveyance had been completed. Alternatively, even if one of these elements were lacking, you could always demonstrate that the period for prescription had passed and that you had legally acquired it through the passage of time.

This action was usually, in the case of movable property, brought in conjunction with the *actio ad exhibendum*, which forced the party in control of the property immediately before the lawsuit commenced to produce the object over which ownership was disputed in a court of law. Once the parties were present, together with the object in question, both had to lead evidence regarding their claim on ownership. The burden of proof lay with the party who did not have possession of the object during the lawsuit. The judge made a ruling and assigned ownership to one of the parties.

Although these were the most prominent property-law remedies in Roman law, it is worth pointing out that other branches of Roman law also provided protection to the owner of the property namely wrongful damage to property and theft. Various praetorian remedies could also be used to protect property. The *cautio damni infecti*, for example, allowed an owner of land to obtain a guarantee from a neighbour whose building work threatened to cause loss whereas the *interdictum quod vi aut clam* could also be used where building work had been undertaken with force or stealth.

As far as the owner's relationship with his neighbours is concerned, Roman law had a few remedies which could be referred to using the collective term 'neighbour law'. The earliest of these, which appear in the Twelve Tables of 450 BCE, regulate the determining of boundaries of land and the unlawful cutting of a neighbour's trees. By the classical period, these initial remedies had been supplemented by a number of others which regulated matters as diverse as the diverting of rainwater, damage caused by dripping eaves, obscured views on account of a neighbour's building activities and various others. The proliferation of remedies affecting neighbours during the classical period is an indication of the increased urbanisation of the Empire and the problems which it caused as well as the increase in agricultural activities where a number of different landowners depended on the shared use of a shared resource such as a river or a lake.

Compared to the remedies which were available to protect ownership, those used to protect possession were more immediate. This reflects the factual nature of possession. Possession was not protected using a legal remedy which had to be brought in the context of a court of law. Rather, the remedies were summary and could be obtained within a short period of time by applying to the praetor. There were three types of interdict. Those to obtain possession for the first time, those to protect existing possession and those to recover prior possession now lost. All that an applicant to the court had to demonstrate in order to succeed with an interdict was that the possession was not obtained through force, stealth or by permission. From the small number of requirements it is clear that the purpose of these remedies was to preserve the status quo, usually as a precursor to a lawsuit about the ownership of the property.

No discussion of the law of property would be complete without some mention of the property-owing capacity of the members of the Roman family. As pointed out in Chapter 2, most of the Roman law of persons and family was written from the perspective of the person at the top of the 'status' pyramid. In Roman terms, this was the head of the household. All other members of the *familia* had reduced/derivative statuses in comparison (as we can see from Gaius' division of persons into those who were legally dependent/independent etc.). Thus the capacity of wives, dependent children and slaves, who all formed part of the *familia*, to own property was in some sense diminished by their status. The rules regarding the capacity of these individuals to own property are fascinating and detailed and provide us with an insight into the Roman legal mind (especially the way they interact with notions of guardianship and tutelage). Given the aim of this book, however, they are best left to more detailed discussions of Roman law.

Suggested further reading

The following books contain more detailed surveys of the Roman law of property:

Bannon, C. *Gardens and Neighbours: Private Water Rights in Roman Italy* (Ann Arbor MI 2009)

Birks, P. (ed.) *New Perspectives on the Roman Law of Property* (Oxford 1989)

Diosdi, G. *Ownership in Ancient and Pre-classical Roman Law* (Budapest 1970)

Finley, M. (ed.) *Studies in Roman Property* (Cambridge 1976)

Rodger, A. *Owners and Neighbours in Roman Law* (Oxford 1972)

Watson, A. *Rome of the XII Tables: Persons and Property* (Princeton NJ 1975)

Watson, A. *The Law of Property in the Later Roman Republic* (Oxford 1968)

3.2. Obligations

The law of obligations covers a vast area of Roman private law. Structurally and conceptually, the various subdivisions of this branch of the law of 'things' are held together by the notion of the obligation. Gaius expresses it in the following manner:

> Inst.Gai.III.88 Let us now proceed to obligations. These are divided into two main species: for every obligation arises either from contract or from delict. [translation: Handouts]

This text, while interesting, does not provide us with a definition of what an obligation is. It merely tells us that the sources of obligations are contract or delict. Thus, by entering into a contract or committing a civil wrong against another person or his property, an obligation arises by law. Why does Gaius not define an obligation? The most plausible reason seems to be one which we have already mentioned earlier, namely that the jurists of the classical period did not feel the need to define concepts since definitions (in the modern sense) did not form part of their mode of reasoning.

Gaius' statement makes it clear that the sources of obligation are contract and delict, but as the following text shows, this mode of classification seems to have been fluid and open to revision:

> Gaius, Golden Words, book 2 Obligations arise either from contract or from wrongdoing or by some special right from various types of causes. [translation: Handouts]

Although the obligation is never defined as such by Gaius, it is important to appreciate that to him a close conceptual link existed between the obligation and the action which had to be used to enforce it (especially under the formulary procedure). Take the following statements:

> Inst.Gai.IV.1-V.1. It remains to speak of actions. Now, to the question how many *genera* of actions there are the more correct answer appears to be that there are two, *in rem* and *in personam*. ... An action *in personam* is one in which we proceed against someone who is under contractual or delictual obligation to us, an action, that is, in which we claim 'that he ought to convey, do, or answer for' something. ... Actions *in rem* are called vindications, actions *in personam*, claiming that there is a duty to convey or do, are called *condictiones*. [translation: Handouts]

Notice the word *genus* here. We have come across it before. Think about what it means in this context. Using this text, we can see that the action used to enforce an obligation was *in personam* and was called a *condictio*. We also get a sense about the content of the obligation namely to 'convey, do, or answer for something'. This is the essence of an obligation in Roman law, succinctly summarised subsequently by the jurist Paul:

> D.44.7.3pr (Paul, Institutes, book 2). The essence of obligations does not consist in making some property or a servitude ours, but binding another person to give, do, or perform something for us. [translation: Handouts]

The first part of our discussions about the law of obligations will focus on obligations created by contract. Gaius tells us the following:

> Inst.Gai.III.89. First let us consider those that arise from contract. Of such there are four *genera*: for an obligation by contract arises either *re* (by delivery of a *res*: real contract), by words (verbal contract), by writing (literal contract), or by consent (consensual contract). [translation: Handouts]

We do not know what motivated Gaius to divide contracts into four groups. It may well be that he created this division personally (but the word *genus* is telling). Be that as it may, for the purposes of his discussed, Gaius wished to stress that it was possible to classify the different contracts which existed at that point in Roman law into four categories on account of a constituent element which bound these groups together. Phrased differently, one could say that the contracts 're' were all classified as such on account of them having the transfer of a thing as a constituent element. Within each of these categories, the Romans identified a number of 'named' contracts. 'Named' contracts are an important issue in Roman law. Unlike modern legal systems which have abandoned most formalities associated with contract law and which recognise a 'general principle of contract' whereby any lawful agreement could be a contract as long as it fulfilled certain general prerequisites, the Roman approach was quite different. The Romans developed individual 'named' contracts (like sale, hire, deposit etc.) each with their own rules. Thus, it is not really possible to discern a law of contract in Roman law. Rather, the Romans had a law of contracts. This insistence on formalism would in time cause problems for the Roman scheme of classification of contracts, but more about this later.

A recurring theme in the Roman law of contracts during our period is the tension between the formalism inherited from the republican period and the need for greater flexibility on account of the expansion of commerce. Furthermore, as with most areas of law, the enactment of the *Constitutio Antoniniana* in 212 CE which gave citizenship to most free inhabitants of the Roman Empire had an effect on the Roman law of contracts, especially those contracts initially only available to Roman citizens. We will now briefly examine the four categories of 'named contracts' together with the individual contracts which resorted under these categories.

Among the verbal contracts, the most important was *stipulatio*. It was a contract created through a solemn, ritual question and answer using specific words. It was of considerable antiquity and its use was initially restricted to Roman citizens. Gaius tells us some of these words that could be used in the following text:

> Inst.Gai.III.92. A verbal obligation is created by question and answer in such forms as: 'Do you solemnly promise conveyance? I solemnly promise conveyance': 'Will you convey? I will convey': 'Do you promise? I promise': 'Do you promise on your honour? I promise on my honour': 'Do you guarantee on your honour? I guarantee on my honour': 'Will you do? I will do.' [translation: Handouts]

Notice that Gaius' account of these words does not include the legally relevant reason why something is being promised or conveyed. In a normal *stipulatio* these would have been included, e.g. 'Do you promise to give me fifteen *denarii* on account of the boar I gave you? I promise.'

Thus, by including the reason for the promise in the question, the *stipulatio* could be adapted to suit a wide variety of situations. The *stipulatio*, more so than any other of the Roman contracts, provides us with a snapshot of the changing nature of Roman commerce during the classical period. Take the following text by Gaius:

> Inst.Gai.III.93. Now the verbal obligation in the form *dari spondes*? *spondeo* is peculiar to Roman citizens; but the other forms belong to the *ius gentium* and are consequently valid between all men, whether Roman citizens or peregrines. And even though expressed in Greek ... they are still valid between Roman citizens, provided they understand Greek. [translation: Handouts]

Here we can see a relaxation of the insistence upon the rule that only certain Latin words could be used for a *stipulatio*. It is interesting to note that Gaius uses the concept of the *ius gentium* (the law of nations) to argue for a relaxation of the rule, most likely on commercial grounds. Roughly a century later in the time of Ulpian, this rule has become even further watered down as we can see from the following text:

> D.45.1.1.6 (Ulpian, *Sabinus*, book 48). It makes no difference whether the reply is made in the same language or in another. For instance, if a man asks in Latin but receives a reply in Greek, as long as the reply is consistent, the obligation is settled. Whether we extend this rule to the Greek language only or even to another, such as Punic or Assyrian or some other tongue, is a matter for doubt. The writings of Sabinus, however, allow it to be true that all tongues can produce a verbal obligation, provided that both parties under-stand each other's language, either of their own accord or by means of a truthful interpreter. [translation: Handouts]

The rules on language were not the only elements of the *stipulatio* that were relaxed during the classical period. We can see from the following two passages by Ulpian that various others elements of the *stipulatio* were relaxed as well:

> D.45.1.1pr-2 (Ulpian, Sabinus, book 48). A stipulation can only be effected when both parties can speak, and therefore neither a mute nor a deaf person nor an *infans* can contract a stipulation: nor, indeed, can someone who is not present, since they should both be able to hear. If, therefore, such a person wishes to take a stipulation,

he does so through a slave who is present and acquires an action on stipulation. Also if someone wishes to be bound by an obligation, let him order it, and he will be bound in respect of the order. 2 If a man asks, 'will you give', and the other replies, 'why not', he will certainly be in the position of being bound, but not if he has nodded assent without speaking. For it is a matter not only of civil but also of natural law that a man who nods assent in this way is not bound: and for that reason it is right to say that a guarantor on his behalf is equally not bound. [translation: Handouts]

During the course of the classical period, the scope of the *stipulatio* was progressively narrowed as the Roman law of contracts developed further and more of the 'named' contracts were recognised. This factor, together with the unique Roman nature of a contract based on a ritual question and answer led to its demise as a form of contracting by the end of the classical period. We can see this from the following text by Ulpian:

D.2.14.7.12 (Ulpian, Edict, book 4). With regard to the clause commonly inserted at the end of a pact, – 'Titius asked, Maevius promised,' – these words are not understood as only making a pact, but as making a stipulation equally well, consequently an action *ex stipulatu* arises on them, unless the contrary effect is expressly proved, that is, that the words were used with the intention of making a bare agreement, and not a stipulation. [translation: Handouts]

Here, the *stipulatio* is nothing more than an afterthought. It is used to provide a ground for litigation where the parties have made a pact (an informal agreement which does not conform to the requirements of one of the 'named' contracts). In fact, one cannot even be sure that the formalities of the *stipulatio* were ever actually undertaken. It may well be that the parties pretended to have undergone a *stipulatio* merely as a formality. Apart from the *stipulatio*, Roman legal sources also mention other forms of verbal contracts (e.g. the formal promise of a dowry), but these were legally insignificant and need not detain us here.

The literal contract which was created by recording debts in your household ledger entries owed to you by other people was still in existence in the first century CE. Gaius tells us how it works:

Inst.Gai.III.128. A literal obligation is created by transcriptive entries. A transcriptive entry is made in two ways: *a re in personam* or *a persona in personam*. 129 It is made *a re in personam* where, for instance, I enter to your debit what you owe me on account of a purchase, a hiring, or a partnership. 130 It is made *a persona in personam* where, for instance, I enter to your debit what Titius owes me, provided, that is, that Titius has assigned you to me as debtor in his place. 131 The entries known as cash-entries are of a different nature. For in their case the obligation is real, not literal, since their validity depends on the money having been paid, and payment of money creates a real obligation. This is why it is right to say that cash-entries create no obligation, but merely afford proof of an existing obligation. 132 It is therefore incorrect to say that even peregrines are bound by cash-entries, because what they are bound by is not the entry itself, but the payment of money; the latter form of obligation is *iuris gentium*. 133 But whether peregrines can be bound by transcriptive entries is questioned with good reason, because this kind of obligation is in a way *iuris civilis*. Nerva held accordingly, but Sabinus and Cassius considered that peregrines as well as citizens are bound if the transcriptive entry is *a re in personam*, but not if it is *a persona in personam*. 134 Furthermore, a literal obligation appears to be created by chirographs and syngraphs, that is to say documents acknowledging a debt or promising a payment, of course on the assumption that a stipulation is not made in the matter. This form of obligation is special to peregrines. [translation: Handouts]

Owing to its cumbersome nature and a decline in the practice of keeping household accounts, it ceased to exist as a contract by the end of the classical period. One can also deduce from Gaius' comment here that the recording of debts in household ledger entries was a peculiarly Roman practice which, when confronted by the accounting practices of non-Romans, struggled to adapt. It may well be that such an accounting practice was not conducive to the demands of Empire-wide commerce.

It is commonly accepted that the 'real' contracts (loan for consumption, loan for use, deposit and pledge) were all in existence by the start of the classical period, even though loan for consumption (*mutuum*) is the only one of this category mentioned in Gaius' Institutes (3.90) (Schulz, *Roman Law*, 519). The reason for this is most likely that, of the four named contracts, loan for consumption had a practical use as a way in which to lend money. Take the following example:

Lupus Carentis said that he personally accepted and will accept from Iulius Alexander 50 denarii which he ought to return to him

without any controversy [place of the transaction]. (*FIRA* III, §120)
[translation: mine]

X, a money-lender, lent out 50 *denarii* to Y for whatever purpose. If X wanted to ensure that he could reclaim the money if Y were to fail to pay it back according to the terms of their agreement, they would have to enter into a loan for consumption. The name of the contract is an indication of its operation. The debtor, Y, acquired ownership of the money by virtue of the loan. He was not obliged to return the exact same coins, but the exact equivalent amount. The money-lender could enforce the repayment of the loan, if the debtor failed to pay according to the agreement, through a legal action known as a *condictio* (for a certain amount of money or things). Curiously, even though the loan for consumption was used for money-lending, it had to be 'in theory' for the return of the amount of money/things only. Thus, one could not charge interest on the amount of money lent (most likely owing to its origin in friendship). As this would not be good financial practice, the Roman jurists developed a legal 'fudge' by adding the interest to a *stipulatio* linked to the contract. This preserved the 'no-interest' idea, while allowing the creditor to obtain interest from the loan. An analogous loan of money for a voyage (*fenus nauticum*) arose during the classical period. Although it appears to be related to loan for consumption, it was treated in Roman legal sources as an independent contract. The most important legal development in the contract of loan for consumption during the classical period was the *Senatusconsultum Macedonianum* of *c.* 50 CE which deprived creditors, who had made loans of money to sons in power, of an action. This meant that money-lenders could not recover these debts through the courts at all, even after the son had become legally independent.

The loan for use (*commodatum*), which shares many of the features of the loan for consumption, was probably the last of the real contracts to emerge. In essence, the parties agreed to an object being lent out gratuitously to be returned at a future point in time. It was recognised in law as a separate contract by the time of the redaction into statute of the Praetorian Edict under the Emperor Hadrian in the first half of the second century CE. No real innovations seem to have been introduced into this contract in the classical period apart from the granting of an action against a ward who had entered into this contract without authorisation.

The contract of deposit, where someone agreed to accept a specific object for safekeeping for a specified period of time, also seems to have been substantially developed by the start of this period (Schulz, *Roman Law*, 518). It remained gratuitous throughout the classical period and the only development was the recognition of the irregular deposit of fungible things (*depositum irregulare*) (*contra* Schulz, *Roman Law*, 519-20).

The contract of pledge (*pignus*) continued to exist and develop alongside its more antiquated form *fiducia* throughout the classical period (Buckland/Stein, *Roman Law*, 431, 474). We have already mentioned this contract before in relation to 'limited real rights'. The main legal developments in the contract of pledge were the recognition of an implied right to sell the object of pledge if the borrower defaulted in the repayment of the loan and certain developments in the right to foreclosure. It also seems that an extension in the scope of the *actio serviana*, the action available to the creditor to enforce the hypothec, occurred in the related contract of hypothec.

Classical Roman law recognised four named consensual contracts, namely sale, letting and hiring, partnership and mandate. Gaius explains the underlying reason which binds this category together:

> Inst.Gai.III.135 Obligations are created by consent in sale, hire, partnership, and mandate. 136 The reason why we say that in these cases the obligations are contracted by consent is that no formality whether of words or writing is required, but it is enough that the persons dealing have consented. Hence such contracts can be formed between parties at a distance, say by letter or messenger, whereas a verbal obligation cannot be formed between parties at a distance. 137 Further, in these contracts the parties are reciprocally liable for what each is bound in fairness and equity to perform for the other, whereas in verbal obligations the one party puts and the other gives the stipulatory promise, and in literal contracts the one party by entering the debit imposes and the other incurs the obligation. [translation: Handouts]

From this text one can see that the two most important elements in this category were consent and reciprocity. Notice also that the extent of the parties' obligations was determined by notions of 'fairness and equity'. These terms allude to the *formula* of the actions which were available in relation to each of the contracts.

Let us take an example of a Roman sale dating from 77 CE and recorded on a papyrus from Egypt to explain how the contract of sale worked:

> Gaius Valerius Longus, knight of the Aprian flank [of the army] bought a black Cappadocian horse for the price of 2600 drachmas from Iulius Rufus, centurion of the twenty-second legion. [description of the horse and an attestation that it is in good health] And should someone evict him [i.e. successfully claim ownership of the

horse] [penalty clause]. Gaius Iulius Rufus says that he has accepted and that he holds the 2600 drachmas from Gaius Valerius Longus the purchaser and that the above-mentioned horse has been trans-ferred to him. [date and place of transaction]. (*FIRA* III, § 136) [translation: mine]

Here we can see that for a consensual sale to come into existence, the parties must have agreed on the object (and its description to avoid any mistake) as well as on the price. The Roman jurists spent much time analysing these elements. Thus, for example, they frequently discussed the types of mistake which could occur in relation to a sale (mistake regarding the person, the object of sale, the price) and whether these would terminate the consent on which the contract was based. Furthermore, they were also interested in the rules relating to the price and finally settled on a number of broad ideas. The price had to be in money, it had to ascertained or at least ascertainable from the agreement and finally it had to reflect the value of the object sold (it could not be a sale for a token price of one *denarius*). This resembled a gift, which to the Romans was never a commercial contract.

Several legal innovations occurred in the contract of sale during the classical period. Rules on risk and error developed during this period as well as further refinement regarding the purchaser's guarantee against eviction and the seller's liability for latent defects. This is particularly evident in the sale of slaves which was governed not only by the general law of sale, but also by specific rules originating from the edict of the aediles, the officials in charge of the marketplace. The edict stated the following:

That part of the edict of the aediles which covers the sale of slaves is phrased as follows: 'Let care be taken that the bill of sale for each slave be written in such a way that it can be known exactly what disease or defect each one has, and which one is a runaway or wanderer, or not innocent of any offence.' (Aulus Gellius, *Attic Nights* 4.2.1) [translation: Shelton §199].

Let us see how these rules translate into contractual practice. Take the following contract for the sale of a slave recorded in Egypt in 129 CE, which we have seen before:

Agathos Daemon, the son of Dionysius and Hermione, who resides in the city of Oxyrynchus, by this document acknowledges to Gaius Julius Germanus, son of Gaius Julius Domitianus, that he accept as valid the handwritten sales contract which they made concerning the female slave Dioscouros, about twenty-five years old and without distinguishing marks. Julius Germanus took possession of her from Agathos Daemon just as she was. She is nonreturnable, except for epilepsy or external claim. The price was 1200 drachmas of silver which Agathos Daemon received in full from Julius Germanus when the handwritten sales contract was made out. For this amount Julius Germanus paid the sales tax on the aforementioned slave. A warranty on this slave has been given by Agathos Daemon according to all the claims made in the sales contract. (P.Oxy. 95) [translation: Shelton §200]

From this contract between a Roman and a Greek, we can see that the parties were careful to record all the details as required by law. Failure to do so presumably meant that the sale could be voided within a certain period of time.

D.21.1.28 (Gaius, Edict of the Curule Aedile, book 1). The aediles, if a seller will not enter into formal verbal contract concerning the matters provided by their edict, promise an action of redhibition [i.e. an action for the return of the property] against him within two months and an action for the buyer's damages within six. [translation: Handouts]

In time, the provisions of the edict were applied to other types of sale as well. We can see the development of this idea in the following two texts:

D.21.1.1pr (Ulpian, Edict of the Curule Aedile, book 1). Labeo writes that the edict of the curule aediles applies just as much to sales of land as to sales of inanimate or animate property. [translation: Handouts]

D.21.1.63 (Ulpian, Edict of the Curule Aedile, book 1). It should be understood that this edict relates only to sales, though to sales not of slaves only, but of everything else. It used to be considered strange that no edict is issued concerning the contract of hire, but the explanation given is that either the aediles never had jurisdiction over this contract, or that matters are ordered otherwise in hiring than in sale. [translation: Handouts]

In the contract of hire there was an increased sophistication of certain aspects of urban and agricultural tenancy during the classical period. Like sale, the contract of letting and hiring provide fascinating glimpses into Roman commercial practice. Take the following two examples. The first is a rental notice from Pompeii scribbled on a wall:

> This lodging is available for rent. [it contains] a dining room with three couches. (*FIRA* III § 144) [translation: mine]

This is not a contract as such. It is merely a notice that the property is available. For a contract of letting and hiring to exist, the parties had to agree on the object to be rented and the price. From the snippets of information (since no rental contract for property has been preserved in its entirety) we know that these contracts could often be quite detailed and could spell out in minute detail what the tenant was permitted and not permitted to do in the rental property. The Roman jurists, in their discussions of this contract, spent much time on these rights and duties of the parties to the contract and also paid much attention to contracts which did not quite fit the mould, but could be said to be either sale or letting and hiring.

The fundamental distinction in the Roman contract of letting and hiring lay between the letting of an object (*locatio conductio rei*) and the letting of the services of a person (i.e. not a slave) (*locatio conductio* of *operae*). Take the following text from a contract for the services of a miner in the Roman province of Dacia dating from 164 CE:

> Flavius Secundinus wrote, at the request of Memmius Asclepi who is illiterate, that he [Memmius Asclepi] lets out his services to the Aurelius Adiutor, manager of the gold mine, from this day in the Ides of November, for seventy *denarii* plus food. ... (*FIRA* III §150) [translation: A. Berger, 'A labor contract of AD 164: CIL, III, P. 948, No. X', *CPh* (1948) 43: 231-42]

This fascinating text provides us with much detail about Roman contractual practice. It also demonstrates how the concerns and pre-occupations of the Roman jurists translated into legal practice. Towards the end of this period certain forms of perpetual lease aimed at provincial land started to develop. Little can be said about this development. It was almost certainly connected in some way to the crisis of the third century CE.

The contract of partnership, which had developed during the Republic, undergoes little change in the classical period. Take the following example:

> Between Cassius Frontinus and Iulius Alexander a money-lending partnership is created .... . [The partnership] has been formed in such a way that whatever profit or loss may arise out of it, they shall bear it in equal portions. (*FIRA* III, §157) [translation: mine]

This text provides us with all the essential elements of the partnership contract. It shows the type of partnership, the date on which it was created and the distribution of profit and loss. During the classical period unequal shares in profit and loss was permitted by law.

The contract of mandate undergoes little change in the classical period. Let us take an example from 148 CE from Egypt in the form of a letter. After the usual salutations the letter states:

> I instruct you by this letter to administer my property which lies in the parish of Arsinoe [a description of all of the tasks which have to be undertaken]. ... [*FIRA* III, §159] [translation: mine]

The letter ends with a very formal exhortation that the writer trusts his agent to fulfil his instructions. By looking at this example of mandate we are able to identify all of the requirements which the jurists discuss in abstract terms. Mandate was an instruction to manage affairs, usually over a distance. It implies a pre-existing relationship of trust between the person sending the instructions and the agent who is tasked with completing them (think for example of the correspondence between Cicero and his trusted friend Atticus). Owing to this pre-existing bond, the jurists insisted that a mandate had to be gratuitous. It could not be undertaken in exchange for money. An interesting area analogous to the notion of mandate which evolved during the late Republic and continued to influence Roman commercial law during the course of the Empire was the use of slaves as business agents (and by analogy also to sons in power). A slave could not be an agent in the way described above as it was not deemed to have legal standing for the purposes of Roman private law. Slaves could nonetheless be useful in commercial dealings, especially where they exhibited business acumen. Thus the praetor devised a number of actions which enabled the slave to operate as a business agent on behalf of his master while at the same time providing assurance to third parties transacting with the slave that the master would honour such debts. Gaius tells us how these actions evolved:

> Inst.Gai.4.70. Firstly, where the transaction has been entered into with the authorisation (*iussum*) of the father or master, the

praetor has provided an action [the *actio quod iussu*] against the father or master for the full amount due (*in solidum*). [translation: Handouts]

So where the slave had full authority to enter into the transaction, he was nothing more than an extension of the master who, for whatever reason (distance/other commitments), could not be present at the transaction. Thus, any debts incurred as a result of the transaction could be enforced in full against the master. Two further actions were eventually added to deal with specific type of authorisation:

Inst.Gai.IV.71. On that same principle the praetor has provided two other actions, the *actio exercitoria* and the *actio institoria* ... . The *actio exercitoria* applies when the father or master has put his son or his slave in charge of a ship ... it has been considered entirely equitable that the action is given for the full amount due. The *formula institoria* applies when a man has put his son or slave ... in charge of a ship or of other business ... this *formula* too is for the full amount due. [translation: Handouts]

One can clearly see that these two actions were introduced to deal with scenarios akin to the one covered by *iussum*. In the case of the ship, one could argue that the distance and the continuous nature of the commercial undertakings which a ship's captain had to engage in may have necessitated the creation of these actions.

This concludes our discussion of the 'named' contracts according to Gaius' scheme. There were of a course a number of other contractual agreements which were recognised by Roman law, but which did not come under this scheme. These are best reserved for a technical manual of Roman law but a brief survey will be provided. Agreements that would be grouped under Justinianic law into the category of quasi-contracts were seemingly in existence by the classical period, but were not yet regarded as a homogeneous category. Quasi-contracts resembled 'named' contracts, but lacked some of the essentials. The existence of innominate contracts during the classical period for long remained a matter of some controversy. Modern scholarly opinion states that although this category did not exist in classical Roman law, the agreements eventually contained therein already existed (e.g. sale or return, barter, settlement of a claim or lease at will) (Diósdi, *Contract*, 49-50, Johnston, *Roman Law*, 78-9). Indeed, the classification of these agreements according to the nature of the performance dates from this period (D.19.5.5pr). The innominate contracts fell into one of two types, either where the agreement resembled an existing contract, but where it was unsure which one or where the agreement resembled a mixture of one or more contract. If one party to such an agreement fulfilled their obligations, an innominate contract came into existence and jurists were prepared to allow ad hoc or factual actions to protect the other party to the agreement. It is evident that these agreements would have had a rather limited existence next to the accepted types of contract and the fact that no attempt was ever made to elevate it into the fourfold division of contract in classical Roman law is an indication of its limited scope of application.

Informal agreements such as pacts were generally unenforceable as contracts during this period, but the classical period witnessed a development in the legal recognition of pacts (Schulz, *Roman Law*, 470-1). Not only was it recognised towards the end of this period that ancillary pacts could vary existing obligations, but the so-called 'clothed pacts' that were unconnected to an existing contract was in the process of being granted legal recognition as unofficial contracts in the post-classical period.

Suggested further reading:

The following works provide a more detailed overview of specific aspects of the Roman law of contracts:

Andreau, J. *Banking and Business in the Roman World* (Cambridge 1999)

Aubert, J.-J. *Business Managers in Ancient Rome* (Leiden 1994)

Buckler, W. *The Origin and History of Contract in Roman Law Down to the End of the Republican Period* (reprint) (Charleston CL 2009)

Diosdi, G. *Contract in Roman Law: From the Twelve Tables to the Glossators* (Budapest 1981)

Kirschenbaum, A. *Sons, Slaves and Freedmen in Roman Commerce* (Washington DC 1999)

Riccobono, S. *Stipulation and the Theory of Contract* (translated from Italian) (Amsterdam 1957)

Watson, A. *The Contract of Mandate in Roman Law* (Oxford 1961)

Watson, A. *The Law of Obligations in the Later Roman Republic* (Oxford 1965)

Zimmermann, R. *The Law of Obligations: Roman Foundations of the Civilian Tradition* (Cape Town 1990)

Delicts

Delicts are civil wrongs which give rise to an obligation at law. This means that they are wrongful actions which have caused loss to the victim and which are not remedied through prosecution by the state, but rather through private civil prosecution by the victim or his family. In the scheme set out in Gaius' Institutes, four named delicts are mentioned. These are theft (*furtum*), robbery (*rapina*), wrongful damage to property (*damnum iniuria datum*) and insult (*iniuria*). Of these, theft and robbery would in modern law be classified as 'crimes' which are prosecuted by the state on behalf of the victim, but to the Romans they were first and foremost civil wrongs which had to be the subject of private litigation. Why did the Romans regard these as private wrongs rather than crimes? The answer to this is not clear. It is conventionally assumed that criminal law was underdeveloped in the Roman Republic, when most of these civil wrongs developed, and that these remedies therefore filled a gap created by the absence of state machinery to prosecute crimes. This is certainly plausible as we see from the sources that during the classical period, as criminal law develops, the Roman jurists begin to comment that alongside private litigation on account of a delict it has also become possible to prosecute the wrongdoer through the criminal courts. With that said, the absence of state machinery and the underdeveloped nature of Roman criminal law might not be the full reason for the development of the Roman law of delict in the sphere of private law. It is also clear that many of the 'named' delicts are uniquely Roman and are intimately related to their under-standing of themselves and their property. Most of the named delicts can in fact be traced back in origin to the Twelve Tables which, if it is indeed no more than an account of the more controversial areas of Roman custom, shows that these delicts are firmly rooted in ancient Roman custom. Gaius' comment on the structure of the Roman law of delicts provides interesting insights as to the origins of these wrongs:

> Inst.Gai.III.182. Now let us pass on to obligations arising from delict, as where theft or robbery is committed, or damage to property is done, or injury to the person. Obligations from these sources all belong to one *genus*, whereas as we have already explained, obligations from contract are distributed among four *genera*. [translation: Handouts]

This statement contains two important pieces of information. First, Gaius mentions only the four 'named' delicts. We know from other legal sources that the praetors had also begun to develop other 'Praetorian' delicts by this time, but since Gaius does not mention them we must assume either that they were still in development or that they fell outside the scope of his book. More importantly, however, Gaius obliquely mentions that obligations arising from delict all belong to one *genus*, unlike obligations arising from contract which belong to four *genera*. What does this mean? Let us take the final part of this sentence first. We have already seen that the Roman jurists divided their law of contracts into four categories (*genera*) in which individual contracts were grouped together based on their most prominent element (handing over of the object, consent etc.). If we assume that this is what Gaius meant with the term *genus* (category), then he is saying that all of the 'named' Roman delicts basically belong to one category, that is, they are unified by one thing. As is typical of Gaius, he does not say what this is, but reading between the lines one must assume that he meant that they are all 'wrongs' (*iniuria*), that is unlawful conduct which generates an obligation on the part of the wrongdoer or his family to compensate the victim for the loss suffered. As we will presently see, the Roman law of delicts had a penal element built into the amount which a victim or his family could claim for the wrong suffered. The penal element was mainly expressed in terms of the size of the claim with double or fourfold the damages being awarded to penalise the wrongdoer for his conduct.

Let us now look at these four delicts in turn. There are two peculiar features of the Roman law of theft. The first is that by the classical period it had become a very broad concept which included not only the actual theft of another's property, but also any dishonest handling of the property of another. This expansion of the concept is mostly likely related to an acknowledgement in law that more people than just the owner could have a legal interest in the property which required protection. Secondly, the Roman law of theft is mostly aimed at claiming financial compensation for the theft rather than the recovery of the object. One would imagine that this narrowed the potential of litigating against a thief, especially those who did not really have any money, but in a patriarchal society in which men were connected by complex webs of patronage and friendship together with the social opprobrium brought about by being convicted of theft (it was one of the *actiones famosae* which brought with it *infamia*, social disgrace) likely made it a particularly useful remedy. As mentioned before, specific rules on theft may be traced as far back as the Twelve Tables. Reconstructions of the Twelve Tables combined with Gaius' statements suggest that the two main forms of theft recognised in this period were manifest and non-manifest theft. Manifest theft seems to have consisted of cases where the thief was caught in the act, while non-manifest theft was everything else (by the time of Gaius there is clearly some debate over the meaning of these terms, see Inst.Gai. III.184-5). Gaius tells us the following about the punishment of manifest theft in the time of the Twelve Tables:

> Inst.Gai.III.189. Under the Twelve Tables the penalty for manifest theft used to be capital. A free man was scourged and then solemnly assigned by the magistrate to him from whom he had stolen; whether by the *addictio* the thief was made a slave, or was placed in the position of a judgment debtor, used to be disputed by early lawyers. A slave, after being similarly scourged, was put to death.
> … [translation: Handouts]

These are very harsh penalties. In both cases, the thief would be scourged (severely beaten/flogged) followed by further penalties. As one can see from Gaius' comment, written in c. 160 CE, he was no longer clear what the exact status of the free thief would be after being assigned to the victim and whether the thief in fact lost his liberty (the most precious commodity in Roman society). The motivation for the killing of the slave thief probably lay both in deterring other slaves from doing the same and also in removing a potential threat from a society based in a small city-state. But what of those cases of theft where the victim had good reason to suspect that he may have been burgled by a specific person but had not caught them in the act? Gaius tells us about this as well. Apparently, the victim could insist on searching the house of the suspected thief:

> Inst.Gai.III.192. The Law of the Twelve Tables … ordains that one wishing to search must do so naked, girt with a *licium* and holding a platter; if he finds anything, the law says it is to be manifest theft. 193 What, it has been asked, is the *licium*? Probably it is some sort of cloth for covering the private parts. The whole thing is ridiculous.
> [translation: Handouts]

Gaius, who is usually interested in legal history, seems dismissive of the ancient practice here. Why should that be? In all likelihood, this procedure had long fallen into disuse, and it is clear from his musings on the term *licium* that he did not really understand what it meant. This can only mean that Gaius found the idea of stripping down to your underwear to search the house of a suspected thief a bit silly. But for all Gaius' scorn over this procedure, it should not be dismissed off hand. The ritual described above (and it clearly is a ritual) may have had a very specific purpose. By stripping down to one's underwear, there could be no suggestion from the suspected thief that the alleged victim had somehow 'planted' allegedly stolen goods in the house in order to satisfy some grudge which he might hold against the victim. Given the seriousness of the penalties for theft in the Twelve Tables, this must have been a serious concern. Secondly, it seems likely that the platter may have been employed to demonstrate the stolen object to the world at large, but this is purely conjecture. It should not be forgotten that in the time of the Twelve Tables there was as yet no clear concept of 'defamation', such as falsely accusing someone of theft. Finally, for non-manifest theft, the penalties were less severe and consisted of damage amounting to double the value of the thing stolen (Inst.Gai.III.190).

From this brief discussion of the rules on theft in the Twelve Tables it should be clear that the concept was a very literal one. Theft, in this period, consisted of the physical carrying off of a piece of movable property owned by another. From these literal foundations, the jurists of the classical period spent much time expanding the concept through their interpretation to adapt to the changes in Roman society. Let us take a look at how this was done. First, there is the issue of defining theft. There are two definitions of theft in Roman legal sources of the classical period. The earlier one is by Labeo, a jurist of the time of Augustus, and the second one is by the jurist Paul, a contemporary of Ulpian who lived during the reign of Alexander Severus in the early third century CE. Let us look at these two 'definitions'

> D.47.2.1pr (Paul, Edict, book 39). *Furtum* (theft), says Labeo, is so called from *furvus*, that is, 'black', because it is committed secretly and in the dark and generally at night; or from *fraus*, as Sabinus says: or from the word to carry (*ferre*) or carry away (*auferre*) or it comes from the Greek, in which language a thief is called *phor*: indeed the Greeks themselves derive their own word from *pherein*. [translation: Handouts]

> D.47.2.1.3 (Paul, Edict, book 39). *Furtum* is the dishonest handling of a thing in order to make gain either out of the thing itself or else out of the use or possession thereof. From such conduct natural law commands us to abstain. [translation: Handouts]

Of these two definitions, most of us will agree that the second one is closer to what we would call a definition in modern terms. The first one seems somewhat speculative as it never really defines what theft it. But to the Roman jurists of the early classical period, the first definition would have been the more comprehensible one. This is because jurists of the early (and even mid) classical period did not see the need to define terms in the way that we see in the definition of Paul. Where a concept required further elucidation, this was done using etymology (as we can see in the first definition). By exploring the etymology (albeit spurious), the jurists formed a 'sense' of the term which was sufficient for their purposes. Such 'definitions' also worked well under the formulary system where the second part of the civil suit was conducted by advocates trained in Roman rhetoric rather than legal dogmatics. So why the need for a second definition towards the end of the classical period? The answer for this most probably lies in the change in court procedure from the formulary procedure to the *cognitio* in which etymological 'definitions' such as the one offered by Labeo were less useful, but a definition which encapsulated the essential elements of the concept served more of a purpose (We will return to this matter later.)

The jurists of the classical period focused on four areas of the Roman law of theft. These are (a) what constituted theft; (b) who could commit theft, and related to this (c) intent to steal, and finally (d) what could be stolen. Let us investigate these with reference to a number of texts. On the matter of what constituted theft, take the following two texts:

Inst.Gai.III.202. Sometimes a man is liable for theft of which he is not the actual perpetrator; we refer to one by those whose aid and counsel the theft has been carried out, for instance a man who knocks coins out of your hands, or obstructs you, for another to make off with them, or who stampedes your sheep or cattle for another to catch them. So the old lawyers wrote of one who stampeded a herd with a red rag. [translation: Handouts]

D.47.2.67.2 (Paul, Plautius, book 7). Where a man maliciously summoned a mule-driver to answer a case in law, and in the latter's absence the mules were stolen, the old lawyers held the man was liable for *furtum*. [translation: Handouts]

In these texts we are not so much concerned with the chronology of the authors, but their references to the 'old lawyers' (*veteres*). This term is usually reserved for lawyers of the republican period and it shows us how the idea of theft evolved. In the Twelve Tables theft only occurred where a movable object had been physically moved by the thief to another location. In time, this requirement was relaxed to include the 'facilitating' of stealing, as in the mule-driver case (notice the similarity here between facilitating theft and 'furnishing a cause of death' under the *Lex Aquilia*). This would eventually mature into the notion of 'interference' which did not require any physical moving of the object stolen.

As for point (b), the Roman jurists were here mostly concerned whether the person who committed the theft appreciated the nature of their actions (think back to the Roman law of persons and family – 'status'). Take the following example:

> Inst.Gai.III.208. Finally be it noted that it has been a question whether a person below puberty commits theft by removing another's thing. Most lawyers hold that, since theft depends on intention, the child is only liable on such a charge if he is approaching puberty and so understands that he is doing wrong. [translation: Handouts]

Closely related to this is the notion of the intention with which theft is committed. We can see the development of this element in a number of texts from the classical period:

> Inst.Gai.III.197. ... [T]heft is not committed without dishonest intention. [translation: Handouts]

> Inst.Gai.III.202. ... But if it is a mere prank without intention of furthering a theft, the question will be whether an *actio utilis* should be given, since even negligence is punished by the *Lex Aquilia*. [translation: Handouts]

> D.47.2.52.20 (Ulpian, Edict, book 37). If a man drives off a stallion belonging to me, and turns him in among his own mares for breeding purposes, and with no other intention, this is not *furtum*, unless there is the intention to steal ... [translation: Handouts]

It could be difficult to assess the intention in some factual situations, especially where some mistake had crept in. The jurists therefore spent some time exploring the effect of mistake on intention and whether there could still be theft if a person believed that he did not have the permission of the owner to take the object, but in fact did. These rules need not detain us here.

As for the object of theft, in the time of the Twelve Tables it appears to have been limited to movable objects. This element was retained even though the jurist Sabinus in the early classical period tried to make a case that land (immovable property) could also be stolen. His view was not supported, most probably because the 'theft' of land could be dealt with under the Praetorian Interdicts and other property-law remedies such as the *vindicatio*.

There were a number of legal actions which could be brought to obtain redress on account of the theft. These were initially only available to the owner of the property stolen, but by the classical period this had changed, no doubt owing to the recognition in the area of property law that more people than just the owner could have an interest in the property:

> Inst.Gai.III.203. The action of theft lies at the suit of one who has an interest in the safety of the thing, though he be not its owner. [translation: Handouts]

There is no doubt that this expansion of the action was linked to the recognition of other forms of theft such as theft of use or enjoyment, as explained in Inst.Gai.III.196. But what were the remedies for theft? We have already seen that there were two actions (one for manifest and one for non-manifest theft) in the Twelve Tables, and that these had different consequences. For manifest theft, the consequence of a successful suit used to be enslavement or death, but Gaius tells us that eventually under praetorian influence it was changed to fourfold damages. Thus, both for manifest and non-manifest theft, the penalty was financial (Inst.Gai.IV.7). At some point, this was expanded:

> Inst.Gai.IV.4. It is true that out of hatred of thieves and in order to multiply the actions in which they are liable, it has become accepted that, in addition to the penalty for double or quadruple, they are liable also for an action on recovery of the thing in the form 'if it appears that they ought to convey', notwithstanding that the action claiming ownership of the thing lies against them as well. [translation: Handouts]

From this text we can see that there could be at least three actions brought against the thief. It should also be mentioned that in Inst.Gai.III.192 there is mention of an action which could be brought to prevent a ritual search of your house to find stolen goods. By the third century CE, criminal proceedings for theft were also possible. Ulpian tells us that this was primarily done to provide a deterrent to people accusing others of theft without any evidence to prove it. A criminal claim of theft did not preclude a civil action being brought as well.

A brief observation may be made about robbery. Although it is mentioned by Gaius in his fourfold division of the 'named' delicts in Roman law, robbery never captured the imagination of the jurists of the classical period in the same way as theft. Our information is sparse and it would seem that the robbery shared many of the elements of theft. Gaius, our main source, reveals that the praetorian action on robbery was introduced under very specific circumstances:

> Inst.Gai.III.219. He who takes another's property by violence is also liable in theft. For who more truly handles another's property against the will of its owner than the one who robs him with violence? Thus he has rightly been described as an outrageous thief. However, the praetor has introduced a special action which lies for fourfold within a year, and after that for simple value. This action is available even if the robbery is of but a single thing of insignificant value. [translation: Handouts]

This text shows the conceptual relationship between theft and robbery. To Gaius, robbery was merely 'outrageous theft'. We can also clearly see that the praetorian remedy specifically introduced was based on policy decisions. It was designed to curtail robbery, irrespective of the value of the object. It is commonly believed that this action was introduced during the last century of the Republic at a time when Italy was in a turbulent political state. It would certainly fit with other remedies introduced during this period such as the *Lex Iulia de Iniuriis* of *c*. 81 BCE which prohibited violent home invasions and dealt with specific examples of physical assault.

Wrongful damage to the property of another, the second named delict, is one of the most fascinating areas of Roman law. Unlike theft, this area of law was governed by a statute, the *Lex Aquilia*, which was enacted most likely sometime in the third century BCE. The origin of this statute is the subject of much speculation and it may have been enacted in response to civil unrest in the fledgling Roman Republic, but other (economic) arguments have also been offered. Whatever the motivation for this statute may have been, it rendered the system of compensation for wrongful damage to property which existed in the Twelve Tables obsolete and replaced them with a short statute which dealt with the matter in a novel manner. The text of this law has not been preserved, but the bulk of juristic commentary on it permits us to make a fairly accurate reconstruction of the text. The law consisted of three short statements, commonly known as chapters. Chapter 1 stated that if anyone should unlawfully kill the slave or four-footed animal classed as cattle, let him be condemned to pay to the owner the highest value of the object in the year preceding its destruction. Chapter 2 dealt with an antiquated form of mandate and fell into disuse when the contract of mandate arose. Chapter 3 stated that for all other things (apart from slaves and cattle) if anyone shall unlawfully cause loss to the property of another through burning, breaking or rendering asunder, whatever the matter in issue shall be worth in the thirty days preceding/next (the text is ambiguous), let him be condemned to pay to the owner.

It does not take much to realise that these two provisions cover vastly different things and cater for different forms of loss. Chapter 1 is essentially concerned with the total destruction of a certain class of property of another (slaves and four-footed animals classed as cattle). In this case, the owner is able to recover the highest value which these objects had in the year before their destruction. Such a method of calculation would inevitably mean that the owner was able to recover more than the mere (objective financial) value of the object at the point of its destruction. This mode of assessing the quantum of the loss has been justified by modern scholars with reference to the penal nature of the Roman law of delict. It is in effect equivalent to recovering twice or four times the value of the object as in the cases of theft in order to punish the wrongdoer for his unlawful conduct. Why slaves and four-footed animals classed as cattle? The statute was enacted in the mid-Republic when these assets would have had significant economic value and thus presumably warranted specific protection. Chapter 3 has a much wider scope. It applies whenever someone has caused wrongful damage to those assets mentioned in chapter 1 and also to all other movable property. This chapter describes the way in which the damage had to be inflicted – through burning, breaking or rendering asunder. Why did the legislator feel it necessary to include these words? Most likely to reinforce the point that the damage to the object had to be severe and not merely a scratch or a dent.

One of the most fascinating areas of the *Lex Aquilia* is its interpretation. Since the text of the statute can be reconstructed with some certainty, it is possible when looking at the sections on wrongful damage to property in the Digest and in the Institutes to gain a picture of the way in which the praetors and the jurists reinterpreted the wording of the statute to cover new situations which were not envisaged by the original drafters. This was primarily done by stating that in a given case (which fitted some, but not all of the requirements of the original law) an *actio in factum* or *actio utilis* would be available. It is sometimes difficult to distinguish from the texts what the difference was, but it may be said that in broad terms an *actio in factum* was given where the specific facts warranted legal relief whereas an *actio utilis* was given when in an analogous situation legal relief was already available. To succeed with the statutory action under the *Lex Aquilia* (the *actio legis aquiliae*), one had to prove a number of elements: (a) wrongful; (b) destruction of/damage to; (c) the object of another; (d) which could be causally linked to the actions or omission of the wrong-doer; and which (e) caused financial loss to the victim. Let us examine how these elements were reinterpreted during the classical period.

The first element is that of wrongfulness. In the original text of the law, the term *iniuria* (without right) is used. During the classical period, this term had come to be reinterpreted to mean 'fault'. Take the following text by Gaius:

> Inst.Gai.III.211. He is deemed to kill wrongfully (*iniuria*) by whose malice (*dolus*) or negligence (*culpa*) the death is caused. There being no other statute which visits damage without fault, it follows that a man who, without negligence or malice, but by some accident (*casus*), causes loss, goes unpunished. [translation: Handouts]

A similar point of view is raised by Ulpian:

> D.9.2.5.1 (Ulpian, Edict, book 18). Now we must … understand *iniuria* here … as something that is done not according to the law (*non iure*), in short, contrary to the law, that is, if one kills negligently (*culpa*): and so the two actions, on the *Lex Aquilia* and for *iniuriae*, sometimes concur, but there will be two assessments of damages, one for loss and the other for insult. We shall therefore take *iniuria* to mean here loss caused negligently (*culpa*) even by one who intended no harm. [translation: Handouts]

While concepts such as 'malice' and 'negligence' are useful to describe the wrongdoer's state of mind when committing the act, it should be appreciated that they are little more than labels that are capable of more specific interpretation based on the facts of the case. Thus, what consti-tuted 'malice' or 'negligence' or 'accident' depended on the facts of the case as well as the case-law which had built up around these concepts and the Roman jurists spent much time debating the intricacies of these terms.

The second element is that of destruction/damage. Here, the jurists paid specific attention to the meaning of 'damage' according to chapter 3. Take Gaius' statement:

> Inst.Gai.III.217. The third chapter deals with all other loss. Accordingly, it provides an action if a slave or a four-footed beast of the class of cattle is wounded, or if a four-footed animal other than cattle, such as a dog, or a wild beast like a bear or a lion, is either wounded or killed. It also gives a remedy for wrongful damage to all other things and to any inanimate things. [translation: Handouts]

In this text, Gaius is clearly giving us an account of how the term should be understood in his time. It has been argued, based on the final sentence, that the scope of chapter 3 was expanded to cover also inanimate things during the classical period (the view of David Daube expressed in his article in 1936 (52) *LQR*, 253-68). This, in turn, had an effect on the mode of calculating the loss under chapter 3, but we will return to this presently. Even before the time of Gaius, it is clear that the jurists of the classical period were widening the interpretation of the word 'damage' in chapter 3. Take the following text by Ulpian in which he recounts the opinion of Celsus, a jurist of the early classical period who lived during the reign of Hadrian (117-138 CE):

> D.9.2.27.15 (Ulpian, Edict, book 18). Of course the Aquilian action, Celsus says, can be brought against a man who adulterates wine or spills it or turns it into vinegar or otherwise worsens it, because even spilling and turning into vinegar are included in the term 'spoiling' (*corrumpere*). [translation: Handouts]

> D.9.2.27.13 (Ulpian, Edict, book 18). The *lex* says *ruperit* (break off). Almost all the older jurists understood the word to mean *corruperit* (spoils). [translation: Handouts]

As one can see from these two statements, the verbs expressing the way in which loss had to be caused of chapter 3 underwent a reinterpretation during the classical period. Whereas before they referred to serious damage (short of destruction) to animate objects, by the classical period these verbs had been reinterpreted to mean 'spoiling' through actions which were less serious. As for the requirement of the 'object belonging to another', the jurists of the classical period debated whether others who were not the owner, but who had some kind of legal interest in the property damaged or destroyed could also use the action (a similar development occurs in relation to theft):

D.9.2.11.6 (Ulpian, Edict, book 18). Now the action on the *Lex Aquilia* belongs to the *erus*, that is, the owner. 9 Julian says that one to whom clothes have been lent cannot bring the Aquilian action if they are torn, but the action belongs to the owner. 10 Julian discusses whether a usufructuary or usuary has the action on the *Lex Aquilia*. I think it is better to be an *actio utilis* in these circumstances. [translation: Handouts]

Ulpian's view (articulated in the final sentence) that the *actio utilis* should be granted shows that he thought that these holders of real rights such as the usfructuary or the usuary should be given an action by analogy as they were in many respects like the owner of the object.

Causation remains one of the most complex areas of the Roman law of wrongful damage to property. The texts show that the jurists of the classical period took a very practical and context-based approach to the idea of causation (as one would expect). This meant that consequence (the loss) had to be traceable to the actions or omissions of the wrongdoer. If the consequence was too remote, no action was given. However, if the consequence was somewhat remote, but close enough to warrant legal relief, actions based on policy or on the facts of the case were awarded. Take the following examples:

Inst.Gai.III.219. It has been decided that there is an action under the statute only when a man has caused loss with his own body; consequently policy actions are granted if the loss has been caused in some other way, for example if one shuts up and starves to death another man's slave or cattle ... [translation: Handouts]

D.9.2.7.6 (Ulpian, Edict, book 18). Now Celsus says it makes a great deal of difference whether a person kills or furnishes a cause of death, seeing that one who furnishes a cause of death is liable, not to the Aquilian action but to an action *in factum*. Thus he mentions the case of a man who gave poison instead of medicine and says that he furnished a cause of death, just like one who holds out a sword to a lunatic. ... [translation: Handouts]

One final point to consider is that of loss. To succeed with any of the actions available under the *Lex Aquilia*, it had to be shown that the owner of the object had suffered loss which could be quantified in money. This excluded cases where the owner could not be said to have suffered loss. Take the following examples:

D.9.2.27.28 (Ulpian, Edict, book 18). And if a man castrates a slave boy, and so increases his value, Vivianus writes that the Aquilian action does not lie, but one should bring the *actio iniuriarum* or sue under the edict of the aediles or for four times the value. [translation: Handouts]

D.9.2.33pr (Paul, Plautius, book 2). If you kill my slave, I do not think that personal feelings should be taken into account, as when someone kills your natural son whom you would be willing to buy for a high price, but only what he would be worth to all the world. Sextus Pedius agrees that the prices of things are taken not in accordance with personal feelings or convenience of individuals, but in a general way. [translation: Handouts]

These two examples show the complexity of a society in which slavery was a daily reality. We are not told why a castrated slave boy is worth more, and in the second text the reference to 'natural children' is to those of children of the owner by a female slave.

The Roman law of insult, another of the named delicts, is a wide-ranging delict which covers both physical assault and non-physical infringement of one's good name, reputation or integrity. The physical element of insult (assault) is commonly viewed as being the earliest form recognised by Roman law. It is present in the Twelve Tables where a mixture of talion and fixed penalties is set to compensate the victim for the assault. Sometime during the mid-second century BCE, the original actions deriving from the Twelve Tables were rendered obsolete when the praetors intervened to create a new action whereby the compensation for insult suffered would be calculated with reference to the circumstances of the case rather than based on the fixed penalties of the Twelve Tables. The motivation for the introduction of this action has long baffled scholars, but in all likelihood the change was necessitated by economic problems which rendered the fixed penalty system less useful. Gaius tells us about the quantification of the loss under this new action:

Inst.Gai.III.224. But the system now in force is different. For the praetor allows us to make our own assessment of the outrage, and the *iudex* (judge) may, at his discretion, condemn in the amount of our assessment or in a lesser sum. ... [translation: Handouts]

During the course of the first century BCE, the general action on *iniuria* created by the praetors was augmented by a number of specific actions. There were four of these: raising a clamour; accosting the virtue of a matron by enticing away her attendant; defamation and *iniuria* inflicted upon slaves. It is generally assumed that these were only classified as *iniuria* during the classical period. Let us look at each of these in turn:

> D.47.10.15.2 (Ulpian, Edict, book 77). The praetor says: 'I will grant an action against anyone who raises an outcry against another contrary to good morals or who causes this to be done.' Labeo says that to raise an outcry amounts to *iniuria*. [translation: Handouts]

The reference to the Augustan jurist Labeo supports the notion that these specific actions were only classified as *iniuria* during the classical period.

The second action, 'accosting the virtue of a matron' could take one of two forms. It consisted either of making uncouth remarks about a matron or by following her around. Take the following three texts:

> D.47.10.15.20 (Ulpian, Edict, book 77). To 'call out' for this purpose is to make improper suggestions or alluring proposals – this is not like raising a clamour, but it is contrary to good morals. [translation: Handouts]

> D.47.10.15.15 (Ulpian, Edict, book 77). … Still, if a woman was not dressed in matronly clothes, anyone who calls out to her or who entices away her chaperone is liable to an action for *iniuria*. [translation: Handouts]

> D.47.10.15.22 (Ulpian, Edict, book 77). It is one thing to call out or accost someone, and another thing to follow them about; for he who accosts a woman attacks her virtue by his speech, whereas he who follows her constantly, even silently, dogs her steps. … [translation: Handouts]

These texts reveal quite a bit about Roman attitudes to women. Given the patriarchal nature of Roman society, the existence of such rules comes as little surprise. According to Roman men, women, respectable women that is, deserve protection. They should not be subject to humiliating 'calls', be followed around or be left without a chaperone (since no respectable woman appeared in public without an attendant). In each case, the facts would be tested against the requirement that the act had to be 'contrary to good morals'.

As for the third action, defamation, Ulpian gives us an account of the wording of the action:

> D.47.10.15.25 (Ulpian, Edict, book 77). The praetor says: 'Nothing shall be done to bring a person into hatred, ridicule or contempt, and if anyone violates this rule, I will punish him according to the facts of the case.' Labeo says this edict is superfluous, for we can anyway bring a general action for *iniuria*: but it also appears to Labeo himself (and this is indeed correct) that the praetor, having examined this matter, wished to make special mention of it, for it seems that when public acts do not have attention specifically drawn to them they tend to be forgotten. [translation: Handouts]

Although the justification given in the final sentence of this text is not overly convincing, one can see from this that during the early classical period jurists such as Labeo questioned the relationship between this edict specifically developed for defamation and the general praetorian action on insult. Ulpian, in the latter part of the classical period, cites Labeo's view with approval. As for *iniuria* inflicted upon slaves, a curious overlap exists between these two delicts. The *Lex Aquilia* provided a remedy for the killing or wounding of a slave done wrongfully. This part of the delict *iniuria* provided a remedy for slaves which had been beaten (*verberare*) or interrogated without the permission of their owners, provided that both these had been done 'contrary to good morals'. Finally, an additional praetorian remedy catered for the 'corruption of slaves', the scope of which seems to have been mainly psychological rather than physical.

During the classical period, the specific cases of *iniuria* was conceptually reformed into one notion, that of contumely (*contumelia*) which included both physical and non-physical acts which were done with the intention to cause insult. This intention became an important point of discussion among the jurists:

> D.47.10.4 (Paul, Edict, book 50) Nor [is it an *iniuria*] if I, intending to strike my slave with my fist, should unwittingly hit you when you were standing nearby. [translation: Handouts]

Conceptual thinking about *iniuria* also led to discussions among the jurists about whether an insult which has been ignored can be said to be *iniuria*, whether those who do not have the capacity to form the appreciation that they are insulting or being insulted can be sued for *iniuria* and whether the delict can be committed vicariously.

No discussion of the Roman law of delict would be complete without mentioning other cases of delictual liability which, although not recognised as one of the four named delicts in classical Roman law, nevertheless existed. The first of these is the category of 'quasi-delicts' which were classified as such only in Justinianic Roman law, but which already existed as individual cases during the classical period. There were four examples of 'quasi-delict', namely (a) the erring judge; (b) liability of the occupant of a house or apartment for loss caused by things which had been hung or suspended above a public walkway; (c) liability of the occupant of a house or an apartment for loss caused by things thrown or poured out of windows; and finally (d) the liability of the innkeepers, the stable keeper or the ship's captain for loss suffered by their clients. This is a perplexing category which combined a number of disparate situations which cause loss. The most commonly accepted rationale is that they are united by the idea of 'loss' which, although not technically the fault of anyone, nevertheless had to be compensated. Thus the legal order assigned liability to a given party. There are, however, other explanations as well.

Another appendage to the law of the delict covers cases of 'noxal'. In certain instances, a slave-owner could restrict his liability on account of the delicts committed by his slaves (for which he was legally responsible) by handing over the slave in ownership to the victim rather than paying the penalty under the law of delict. Related to this idea was the notion of liability for damage caused by animals. Under Roman law, the owner of the animal could be held liable for the loss provided it could be shown that the animal had acted out of character. Furthermore, a specific rule of the aediles dealt with liability for damage caused by wild animals which had been kept near a public road. To these may be added examples of delicts created through praetorian innovation. These include defences against acts entered into by extortion or through fraud as well as matters such as the corruption of slaves. The rules on these are detailed and are best investigated in works which contain more detailed accounts of Roman law.

Suggested further reading

Frier, B.W. *A Casebook on the Roman law of Delict* (Oxford 1989)
Descheemaeker, E. *The Division of Wrongs: A Historical and Comparative Study* (Oxford 2009)

3.3. Succession

The Roman law of inheritance conceptually formed part of the law of 'things'. To the Roman legal mind, the law of inheritance was concerned with the transfer of things in a broad sense, either through a valid will or, in the absence of a valid will, through specific legal rules which were designed to benefit the remaining family of the deceased. This is one area of Roman law where the importance of the *familia* is more evident than anywhere else. Furthermore, the law's preoccupation with the transmission of the assets of the *familia* from father to first-born son shows the importance of *agnatio* in Roman law. It goes without saying that the law of inheritance was primarily written for those who had assets of which they wished to dispose after their death. It was perhaps less important to those who did not have much to leave to the next generation, but in this respect Roman law is no different from modern law.

Given this natural divide within the law of inheritance between testamentary and intestate succession, it seems prudent to start with the law of testate succession, that is where a valid will existed. Let us take the following example of a will from *c*. 142 CE.

> Antonius Silvanus, *eques* ... made a will. Let Marcus Antonius Satrianus, my son, be my heir of all my property (military and domestic). Let all other parties be disinherited. Let him accept my inheritance in the next 100 days; should he not do so, let him be disinherited. Then, in the next degree, let Antonius ... my brother be my heir and let him accept my inheritance in the next 60 days. I give and legate to him, if he does not accept my inheritance, 750 silver denarii. I hereby appoint Antonia Thermutha the mother of my above-mentioned heir as general agent (*procurator*) of all of my military goods with a view to collect and recover all of my property. [The testator then appoints one of his military colleagues as the tutor of his son and endows him with an amount of money. He also gives legacies of cash to his wife and to the camp commander.] After my death, my slave Cronio, if he has delivered everything correctly and has handed over to my heir mentioned above or to the agent, I wish him to be freed and to be given a twentieth of my estate. [This is followed by a number of formal announcements that the will has been duly drafted and witnessed]. (*FIRA* III, §47) [translation: mine]

The first point to mention about Roman wills was that they were highly formal documents which had to be drawn up in accordance with the formalities described by law. Physically, a will consisted of a papyrus scroll or a wax tablet which was sealed after the testator had completed it and which was then kept securely along with the other important documents of the testator, usually in the strongbox which was located in the home. Upon the death of the testator, the will was ceremonially unsealed and the wishes of the testator made known to the family. Usually, as can be seen from the example above, one person inherited the bulk of the estate (both assets and debts) and the rest of the family was explicitly disinherited. This person was also usually tasked with fulfilling the other wishes of the testator as expressed in the will such as the payment of legacies.

Anyone who had Roman citizenship could make a will once they had reached the age of puberty, but certain classes of people *alieni iuris* (esp. minors and women) needed further authority before they could validly make a will (here the general rules of guardianship and tutelage applied). Gaius states the following:

> Inst.Gai.II.114. And so, if we are asking whether a will is valid, we must first of all consider whether the person who made it had the capacity to make a will ... [translation: Gordon/Robinson]

> Inst.Gai.II.118. Moreover, notice that if a woman under guardianship makes a will, she should have her guardian's authorisation; otherwise the will is not effective by state law. ... [translation: Gordon/Robinson]

Of course, after 212 CE, any free citizen in the Roman Empire could make a will according to Roman law, although it is clear from parts of the Empire where sophisticated legal orders existed prior to Roman occupation that local inhabitants often made wills according to their own laws rather than Roman law. With that said, if you wanted a solution offered by Roman law it was better to use Roman law rather than local law. Who could inherit under a will? Virtually anyone, even slaves, provided that such a testamentary bequest complied with the rules of inheritance.

We will explain these rules using the example of a Roman will provided above. The will contained the final wishes of the testator as to what should happen to his property after his death. It was therefore very important that it should contain no ambiguities and that the wishes of the testator could be clearly interpreted from the will (since he or she could not be asked what they had meant). This may explain why the Roman jurists placed such emphasis on the formalities attached to the writing, sealing and eventual opening of the will. By the time the will above was drafted, it had become customary to create a written will (the older procedure dating from the Twelve Tables permitted a verbal will in front of witnesses using the ritual of *mancipatio*, see Inst.Gai.II.104). Gaius tells us about the form of will which existed during his time:

> Inst.Gai.II.103. ... But the present procedure is quite different from the former practice. ... Nowadays, however, one person is appointed heir by the will, and the legacies are charged on him: ... [translation: Gordon/Robinson]

The main clause in the will (which normally had to be stated at the top of it) was who would be the principal heir (see D.28.6.2.4 (Ulpian, Sabinus, book 6) for a controversy about the matter). Without this clause, the will was invalid. He was the person who inherited the bulk of the estate (both debts and assets). Usually, as can be seen from the example above, this would be the oldest son of the deceased, thereby reinforcing the idea of *agnatio* as the principle on which the Roman law of persons and family operated. (Sons who became legally independent upon the death of their father were called *sui heredes*, see D.28.2.11 (Paul, Sabinus, book 2).) Gaius tells us about strict legal rules in this regard:

> Inst.Gai.II.123. Again, someone with a son within his power must be sure to appoint him heir or to disinherit him specifically. If he passes him over in silence, his will becomes a nullity. ... [translation: Gordon/Robinson]

Failure to make explicit provision for a son in power was fatal to the will and the rules of intestacy applied. In the case of the will of Antonius Silvanus above, the testator awards all of his goods, both domestic and in the military camp, to his son. In the same clause he disinherits anyone else (These could be catered for through smaller bequests such as legacies or *fideicommissa*, see D.28.1.28 (Ulpian, Edict, book 57).) The principal heir is given a certain period to accept the inheritance formally. Take the following example of formal acceptance from 170 CE:

> It is attested by the girl Valeria ... through her procurator Lucius Valerius Matidius and her brother Plutinius Antinoensius that she has formally accepted the inheritance of her mother Flavia Valeria and that she is her heir according to the will. [Date and place of drafting plus signatures of witnesses]. (*FIRA* III, §60) [translation: mine]

As we can see from the will of Antonius Silvanus, should the heir fail to accept the inheritance by the end of the period, he is formally disinherited according to the will and replaced by the next in line. This is known as substitution (see Inst.Gai.II.174-5). The heir next in line is his brother who is also given a specific period of time to accept the inheritance. If he fails to do so by the end of the period, he is formally disinherited, but granted an amount of money as a legacy (I give and legate …). This practice of substitution is the law of the time according to Gaius:

> Inst.Gai.II.164. Outside heirs are usually required to make a formal declaration of acceptance (*cretio* in Latin), that is, a limit is imposed on the time they have to think the matter over; either they accept within the fixed time or if not, at the end of that time they are displaced. … 170 Now, all declarations have a fixed time limit. A tolerable period for this has been taken as a hundred days. [translation: Gordon/Robinson]

The rest of the will of Antonius Silvanus contains a number of provisions. These are instructions which the testator gave to his remaining family. Notice how he instructs someone to act as a *procurator* (general agent) who is tasked with seeing that all of his property is accounted for. Also, notice how the testator uses the will to set free some of his slaves and to provide them with some property. (It was also possible to appoint a slave as heir with a bequest that he be freed and accept the inheritance, see Inst.Gai.II.185-6) Finally, notice how carefully the clauses at the end of the will have been constructed to show that the will was drafted according to the formalities of Roman law and duly witnessed by the correct number of witnesses as prescribed by law.

Apart from the matters specifically highlighted in this will, legal sources show that other matters related to testamentary succession occupied the minds of the jurists. These include matters such as whether a person's estate can be disposed of partly through the rules of testate and partly through the rules of intestate succession; what form of words the legacies included in a will must have (these rules are quite detailed and are best left for a textbook on Roman law); whether the principle of universal succession could be circumvented by leaving the bulk of the estate to individuals using legacies (it was settled that it could not, see the *Lex Falcidia* of 40 BCE); the use of codicils created after the will had been drafted and finally the use of *fideicommissum*, a type of trust whereby money or goods were given to one person in the will, but with the instructions to use it to the benefit of other members of the surviving family (see D.31.77.12 (Papinian, Responses, book 8) for example). Here we have an example of a codicil from 175 CE:

> ... I ask that you erect a monument worthy of my youth for me. ...
> (*FIRA* III, §56) [translation: mine]

While there can be no doubt that many of the finer points regarding these issues were theoretical matters which piqued the interest of the jurists on a conceptual level, it should also be borne in mind that the Roman jurists were actively involved in drafting wills and in providing legal advice to praetors, judges and legal representatives of litigants. Thus, the issues which they discuss in relation to testamentary succession must have a 'real' element as well and thus provide us with a snapshot of some of the most common issues surrounding the rules of testamentary succession in Roman law. This can be seen, for example, in the procedure which developed in the late Republic whereby those who are deemed *sui heredes* (the meaning of this term will be explained below) could challenge a will in the court of the praetor if they felt that they had been wrongly passed over. This process, known as the *Querela inofficiosi testamenti*, which took place in front of the praetor, essentially entailed that the will should be overturned and that the rules of intestate succession should be applied to the estate.

The rules of intestate succession are designed to operate where no will has been made or an existing will has been found not to comply with the formalities set by the Roman law of succession. In essence, it contains a number of rules stating which groups or classes of people should inherit upon the testator's death. The basic principle underlying these rules is that of blood relationship thought the male line. Thus, the first group to inherit was called the *sui heredes*, that is, anyone who would become *sui iuris* by virtue of the death of the testator, typically his sons.

> Inst.Gai.II.152. There are compulsory heirs, immediate and compulsory heirs, and outside heirs. ... 156 The immediate and compulsory heirs are, for instance, a son or daughter, also grandchildren through a son and so on down the line, who were within the paternal power of the deceased at his deathbed. ... 157 These heirs are called immediate, the testator's own heirs, because they come from inside the family and are in a certain sense thought of as owners [of the estate] even while their parent is alive. ... They are called compulsory because they have no other choice in the matter. Whether under a will or not, they become heirs automatically. 158 But the praetor

gives them a right to stand off from the estate so that it is the parent's property which is sold up. ... 161 All other heirs, not being within the testator's paternal power are called outsiders. ... 162 Outsiders have a choice whether to accept the estate or not. ... [translation: Gordon/Robinson]

Where no *sui heredes* existed, the rules of intestate succession dictated that the next class of people to inherit would be the *proximi agnati*, that is those persons related to the testator through *agnatio*, blood relation through the male line. These would be the brothers of the testator or if none existed, his uncles. Finally, if none of these existed, the inheritance would go to the clan to which the testator belonged. Two observations may be made about these rules. First, it is clear that they were drafted, much like the rules of testate succession, to ensure that the bulk of the estate went to the nearest blood relatives of the testator. This reinforces the importance of *agnatio* and *familia* to the Romans. Secondly, certain classes of people are notable by their absence: the rules of intestate succession do not mention spouses or emancipated children at all.

During the course of the classical period, the rules of intestate succession which had developed out of the *ius civile* were slowly altered by the praetor. Since the praetors could not circumvent the civil-law rules, they developed a system of praetorian succession whereby interested parties could apply to the praetor's court for 'possession of the goods' which would enable them to claim the inheritance (it operated like an interdict). The praetorian rules on intestate succession did not alter the civil-law rules. It merely adapted them slightly to take account of classes of persons who, under the civil-law rules, were largely ignored when it came to succession (see D.38.6.1.1-2 (Ulpian, Edict, book 44) for an account of these rules). The rules were as follows. In the first line, all legitimate children could inherit, whether emancipated or not. In the second degree, everyone who would could have inherited under civil law (blood relatives, etc.). In the third degree, all blood relatives whether through the male or the female line. In the fourth degree, the surviving spouse, and finally, if none of these existed, the state. The development of these rules clearly shows the main contribution of praetorian law to the Roman law of succession. Whereas the old civil-law rules were largely concerned with the transfer of property through universal succession, the praetorian rules were more concerned with ensuring that the surviving *familia* should have the benefit of the testator's estate where a will did not exist or had failed on account of a lack of formality.

Suggested further reading

Frier, B.W. and McGinn, T.A.J. *A Casebook on Roman Family Law* (Oxford 2004)

Tellegen, J.W. *Roman Law of Succession in the Letters of Pliny the Younger* (Zutphen 1982)

Tellegen-Couperus, O.E. *Testamentary Succession in the Constitutions of Diocletian* (Zutphen 1982)

Watson, A. *Rome of the XII Tables: Persons and Property* (Princeton NJ 1975)

Watson, A. *The Law of Succession in the Later Roman Republic* (Oxford 1971)

Chapter 4

'Actions'

Gaius, in his discussion of the law of actions, begins with an account of the different types of actions found in Roman law of the classical period. We have already come across many of these in our discussion of the various branches of Roman private law. Gaius summarises it as follows:

> Inst.Gai.IV.1. ... If we should ask how many classes (*genera*) of actions there are, the better view is that there are two, real (*in rem*) and personal (*in personam*) ... 2 A personal action is one which we raise when we sue someone who is under an obligation to us, either contractual or delictual. That is when we claim in our principal pleading that 'there is a duty to give, to do, to fulfil'. 3 A real action is where we claim either that some corporeal thing is ours, or that some right is available to us, for instance a right of use or of usufruct ... . 6 Sometimes we raise an action solely for restoration, sometimes solely for penalty, at other times for both a thing and the penalty. [translation: Gordon/Robinson]

After setting out the different types of action, Gaius proceeds to tell us about their history:

> Inst.Gai.IV.11. The actions used by the old lawyers were described as actions in the law, either because they were set out in statutes, since at the time the Praetor's edicts, which introduced numerous actions, were not yet in use – or because they were precisely adjusted to the words of statutes, and were accordingly observed as if they had been statutes. ... 30. But gradually all these actions in the law fell into disfavour. ... Therefore, by the Aebutian Act and the two Julian Acts these actions in the law were swept away and the system of litigating by means of specially drafted phrases, that is by formulas, was introduced. [translation: Gordon/Robinson]

To understand Roman litigation, one must first appreciate that all litigation, whether in Roman or in modern law, is based on ritual. The entire court process, from summons to the enforcement of the court's verdict, is based on a set of prescribed actions and time-periods within which these actions have to be performed. Once this basic fact is understood, Roman litigation becomes much clearer. But before the process can be examined, a few general observations are required. The Roman law of civil procedure (if it is possible to call it that) can be traced back as far as the Twelve Tables. The procedure described there was highly ritualistic and only available to those who held Roman citizenship. Initially, this procedure would have taken place in front of the consuls who acted as judges, but after the creation of the praetorship in 367 BCE this office was tasked with the administration of justice in Rome. Following the successful conclusion of the Second Punic War against Carthage and with the settlement of many non-citizens in Roman territory, a need arose to accommodate the legal problems of non-citizens. A second praetorship was created, tasked with administering justice between non-citizens. It has been said that the procedure developed in this court was not bound to the rituals laid down in the Twelve Tables and thus proved more flexible. In time, this caused discontent and in *c*. 150 BCE, by virtue of statute (the *Lex Aebutia*), Roman citizens were permitted to use the more flexible procedure, known as the formulary procedure, which had evolved in the court of the peregrine praetor. By the end of the republican period, the formulary procedure had become the standard procedure used in Roman civil courts. The old procedure deriving from the Twelve Tables was formally abolished by August in 17 BCE by way of statute (the *Leges Iuliae iudiciorum privatorum et publicorum*).

> Inst.Gai.IV.30. But all these *legis actiones* gradually became unpopular. For the excessive technicality of the early lawyers was carried so far that a party who made the slightest mistake lost his case. So by the *Lex Aebutia* [second century BCE] and the two *Leges Iuliae* [17 or 16 BCE] they were abolished, and litigation by flexible pleadings, that is by *formulae*, was established. [translation: Handouts]

This discussion will therefore focus primarily on the formulary procedure as it existed in the classical period.

It is important to remember that for much of the classical period, the formulary procedure existed alongside a newer bureaucratic procedure (*cognitio*) which had been introduced during the early years of Augustus' reign. This process was initially confined to certain areas of the law as decreed by the emperor, but in time it came to merge with the formulary procedure so that by the end of the period under discussion it had almost replaced it entirely. The official abolition of the formulary procedure in the first half of the fourth century CE must also have affected the way in which the idea of the *formula* was approached by the courts. Take the following statement:

C.2.57.1. Emperors Constantinus and Constans to Marcellinus. Legal formulas, with the snares of their syllables laying a trap for the acts of all shall be completely abolished. Given January 23 (342). [translation: Blume]

What does this mean? It is difficult to tell. It is interesting to note, however, that a similar justification was used for the abolition of the actions-at-law in favour of the *formula* during the reign of Augustus. Why did the formulary procedure go into decline? The reasons are twofold. First, the expansion of the imperial bureaucracy, which favoured this form of procedure, caused it to be used more widely and in more areas of Roman private law. In second place, the formulary procedure was never applied in the provinces of the Roman Empire. In most provinces which had been created after the fall of the Republic, the bureaucratic process was the standard form of civil procedure (except where the local legal culture was so sophisticated that the Romans left it intact). For the purposes of our discussion, therefore, attention will chiefly be paid to the formulary procedure with certain comments about the bureaucratic process.

Before looking at the procedure, let us first look at the court itself. The idea of a purpose-built room in which a court sits is a medieval rather than a Roman notion. To the Romans, the court existed when the officials and the parties were present and the court had been formally convoked. This could take place in the open, but in time it became customary to hold hearings (in Rome) in the forum or in purpose-built *basilicae* which surrounded the forum. The formulary procedure consisted of two separate stages. The first stage occurred in the court of the praetor. Once this part had been concluded, the second stage in front of one or more judges took place. In most cases, a period of time would elapse between the first and the second stage. The court of the praetor sat only on days when the courts were open (*dies fasti*) and operated from early morning to early evening. It consisted of a raised platform on which the praetor sat in his chair of office. Behind him stood his attendants who carried the symbols of his constitutional power (a ceremonial axe and a bundle of sticks). He may also have had a council of assistants (sometimes lawyers) who sat in front of him on a lower level (although whether the jurists had such a formal role under this procedure is debated). Facing him stood (or sat) the parties and their representatives surrounded by a crowd of onlookers known as the *corona*. This was the Roman courtroom. The same set-up was used in the second stage where the place of the praetor was taken by a single judge or a panel of judges. Since judges did not wield constitutional power, they did not have attendants. Unlike the court of the praetor, the court of the judge could sit on any day (whether *dies fasti* or not), but it could not sit during days when public games were held (Greenidge, *Legal Procedure*, 137).

In order to start litigation in Roman law, the plaintiff (the person wishing to litigate) had to summon the defendant to appear in front of the praetor. This could be done in a variety of ways, but the underlying notion, inherited from the ritualistic procedure of the Twelve Tables, was that summons was essentially a private process. The plaintiff had to make sure that the defendant came to court and the state did not assist the plaintiff directly in ensuring that this happened. The oldest form of ensuring that the plaintiff appear in court was by using 'self-help'. The Twelve Tables permitted the plaintiff under certain circumstances to use force to compel the defendant to appear (as can be seen from Horace, *Ode* 1.9). Although this option was still available during our period, it had by then been sidelined by two more common ways of notifying the defendant of the impending lawsuit. The first of these was to send the defendant a notification of the intended lawsuit and to invite him to appear on a specified day at the court of the praetor. To ensure that parties took this seriously the Praetorian Edict contained a measure of compulsion:

Inst.Gai.IV.183. Finally note that someone who wishes to take proceedings against another person must summon him at law (*in ius vocare*) and that the person summoned incurs a penalty under the Praetor's Edict if he does not come [translation: Handouts]

In second place, and related to the first, the defendant's appearance could be secured using a formal promise backed up by security (usually a sum of money). This promise was called a *vadimonium*, and if the defendant contravened the promise he would forfeit the security. The formal promise was commonly used where a matter had been deferred from another court. It is important to remember that the formal promise did not replace the act of summons. The two procedures operated in tandem. The formal promise was merely a means to secure the presence of the defendant and we know from examples of it that the parties often agreed to appear in the vicinity of the court near a landmark, say a statue of the emperor in the forum. Once they had met at the appointed place and time, ritual summons could take place.

Once this had been done, the parties could then proceed to the court of the praetor to commence the first part of the lawsuit. The parties had to wait their turn until such time as the praetor was free to deal with their case. If it became apparent that too many litigants had appeared at his court and that he would not be able to deal with everyone's claim on the day, the praetor would by the afternoon issue a blanket order instructing those litigants whose cases had not yet been heard to come back on the next court day.

Assuming that the praetor could see the parties on the day, a number of legal issues had to be resolved in his court before the matter could progress to a full civil trial in front of the judge. Some of these issues were procedural, others substantive, but to the Roman legal mind these two things were often the same. The first thing to consider was whether the parties could in fact appear before the praetor. The Digest title *De postulando* (concerning appearances in court) (D.2.4) contains an account of the section of the Praetorian Edict which effectively barred some persons either from being representatives for others or from appearing as litigants. Many of these restrictions related to the status of the person, namely either because they were tainted with infamy on account of a previous judgement or because they were *alieni iuris*. It is also interesting to note that in the *Lex Irnitana* (chapter 84), restrictions were placed on the type of lawsuit that could be heard at a local level. If, upon investigation by the local court, it was found that the matter had to be deferred to a different court, then the case was at an end and the parties made a *vadimonium* (a formal promise) to appear, say in Rome, to take the matter to the appropriate court. Once it had been established that the parties could appear in front of the praetor, the legal basis of the claim then had to be investigated.

To sue under Roman law of the classical period, one had to show that one had a legal claim to do so. This legal claim had to be founded either in the original *ius civile* or in the more recent *ius honorarium* developed through praetorian intervention. By the advent of the classical period, one way of demonstrating that one had a legal claim was with reference to the Praetorian Edict:

> D.2.13.1pr (Ulpian, Edict, book 4). Whatever action a person wants to bring, he must state its nature (*edere actionem*) .... 1 The word 'state' (*edere*) includes the making of a copy [by the defender], or expressing the whole case in a written statement (*libellus*) and giving him it, or dictating it. Labeo says that a person states his case when he takes his opponent up to the praetor's album and points out

what he is going to dictate, or tells him the one he wants to use. [translation: Handouts]

We have already seen that the Praetorian Edict contained stock 'formulae' which set out the skeleton of a legal claim and which could then be filled in by the parties with reference to the facts of the case. It was the main task of the praetor to investigate the matter to see whether the plaintiff did, in fact, have a legal claim based either on the civil law or on the Praetorian Edict. In more complex cases where the parties did not base their claim on existing law, the praetor also had to decide whether he was prepared to extend the existing law by analogy (thereby granting an *actio utilis*) or by granting legal relief based on the specific set of facts presented to him (by granting an *actio in factum*). The *formula* contained all of the essential elements of the lawsuit. Let us look at its parts:

> Inst.Gai.IV.39. These are the parts (*partes*) of a *formula*: a *demonstratio*, an *intentio*, an *adiudicatio* and a *condemnatio*. 40 A demonstratio is the part of a *formula* inserted at the beginning to show the subject-matter of the action, as in this part of a *formula*: 'Whereas (*quod*) Aulus Agerius sold the slave to Numerius Negidius' ... 41 An *intentio* is the part of a *formula* in which the pursuer defines his claim, as in this part of a *formula*: 'If it appears (*si paret*) that N.N. ought to pay (*dare oportere*) A.A. 10,000 sesterces' ... or again; 'If it appears that the slave belongs to A.A. by Quiritary right (*ex iure Quiritum*)' ... 43 A *condemnatio* is the part of a *formula* which gives the *iudex* power to condemn or absolve the defender, as in this part of a *formula*: ... 'Condemn, *iudex*, N.N. to A.A. for a sum not exceeding (*dumtaxat*) 10,000 sesterces. If it does not so appear, absolve him' [translation: Handouts; A.A. = Aulus Agerius, is the stock name used by the Roman jurists to describe the plaintiff and N.N. = Numerius Negidius, the stock name for the defendant]

Having described the various parts of the *formula* and their functions, let us look at two examples:

> Let Titius be *iudex*. If it appears that N.N. ought to pay A.A. 10,000 sesterces, if there was and is no fraud on A.A's part involved in the matter, condemn, *iudex*, N.N. to A.A. for 10,000 sesterces. If it does not so appear, absolve him. [translation: Handouts]

Let Titius be *iudex*. Whereas A.A. sold N.N. the slave in question, which is the subject of this action, whatever N.N. on that account ought to convey or do for A.A. in good faith (*dare facere oportere ex fide bona*) condemn, *iudex*, N.N. to A.A. for that sum. If it does not so appear, absolve him. [translation: Handouts]

Notice that these two *formulae* are different. The one starts with 'if it appears that …' and the other begins with 'whereas …'. This is because the nature of the claim is different. In the first case it is for a fixed sum, whereas in the second case it is left to the discretion of the judge to decide the amount of the condemnation. The text above describes the stock elements of the *formula*, but it should not be forgotten that the defendant could add his counterclaims or defences to the *formula* as well during the first stage of the lawsuit in front of the praetor (such as the defence of fraud which appears in the first example of the formula above 'if there was no fraud …'). Once the praetor was satisfied that the plaintiff had a legal claim that could be framed in terms of an *actio* and both parties were satisfied with the claims and counterclaims or defences inserted in the document, a judge was chosen.

Notice how in the *formula* the name of the judge is inserted at the start. This is an indication that the *formula* as fleshed out by the parties in front of the praetor was in essence an instruction to the judge to decide the matter according to the *formula*. To be a judge in Roman law one needed to fulfil a number of requirements (mostly of property and status). Judges as a rule did not have expert legal training, but they were sometimes assisted by a counsel of experts and could also, as a passage from Aulus Gellius (*Attic Nights* 14.2) shows, take advice from philosophers and lawyers on a point of law. In the case of Rome, those who were eligible to become judges were first examined by the praetor. If they were found suitable, they had to swear an oath that they would fulfil their duties to the best of their abilities. Once this had been completed, their names were entered into an album which contained lists of names. It was the preroga- tive of the parties to choose their own judge (the plaintiff starting first and the defendant having the right of veto) until the parties had settled on a candidate. If they could not, one was assigned to them by the praetor. Once a judge had been chosen, his name was entered at the top of the expanded formula. This then concluded the first stage of the lawsuit and it was said that 'joinder of issue' had occurred. The consequences of this moment for the civil suit are explained as follows:

C.3.9.1. The Emperors Severus and Antoninus to Valens An issue has not been brought to trial (*in iudicum deducta*) if there has only been an initial presentation of it or a preliminary hearing on the type of action involved. For there is a great difference between joinder or issue (*litis contestatio*) and the stating of an action (*actio edita*). Issue has been joined only when the *iudex* begins to hear the case as it is presented in the statement of the claim. (*narratio negotii*) [202 CE] [translation: Handouts]

That meant that the parties were now bound to take the matter to the second stage and were bound by the judgement of the court. After the lapse of a period of time, the parties would reconvene with the judge to begin the second stage of the lawsuit.

At this point, a few observations about representation are required. One feature of the formulary procedure is that the parties could be represented by others and therefore did not always have to be present in court. This could be useful, especially in cases where a case had to be deferred to Rome for a hearing. Representation was possible in both stages of the civil suit under the formulary procedure. The normal rules regarding the status of the representative applied, but specific attention has to be paid to the category of persons under the Edict *de postulando* who could not act as representatives in a court of law. Roman legal sources speak of two types of legal representative. The *procurator* (or general agent) was appointed by the party only informally. He had to provide security at the start of his appearance and, if the party whom he represented lost the case and was condemned by the court to pay an amount of money, the *procurator* had to pay it. The *cognitor* (or litigation agent) was appointed formally using the contract of mandate in the presence of another person. If a *cognitor* lost the case, the party who had instructed him was liable for the payment of the court judgement. It has been suggested that the distinction between these two types of legal representatives became blurred during the classical period.

On the appointed day, the parties and their representatives convened together with the judge to conclude the second stage of the civil suit. The aim of this stage of the lawsuit was to convince the judge, using the facts of the case, that he had to find either in favour of the plaintiff or the defendant. As one can see from the *formulae* described above, the judge had a rather narrow scope, he could only condemn or absolve (a third option – 'not proven' was available, but this is not mentioned in the *formula*). Since the judge did not have expert legal training, it is commonly said that this stage of the trial did not proceed using technical legal arguments (but this remains disputed). Rather, the representatives of the parties used rhetoric (the Roman equivalent of the law of evidence) to prove their client's case. Once both parties had brought evidence and had put forward their carefully constructed arguments using the conventions of rhetoric, the judge had to make a decision. Under the formulary procedure the court's judgement was always expressed in terms of money:

> Inst.Gai.IV.48. The *condemnatio* in all *formulae* which have one is framed in terms of a money valuation. So even where the claim is for corporeal thing, such as land, a slave, a garment, gold or silver, the *iudex* condemns the defender not for the actual thing, as was the practice in early days, but for the amount of money he values it at. [translation: Handouts]

Where the lawsuit concerned the recovery of a specific object, a judgement in money would obviously not be preferable. Thus, to circumvent this problem, it was agreed that the parties could insert an 'arbitration clause' into the *formula* whereby the money judgement of the court would only be invoked if the party who had lost the lawsuit did not return the object.

Once the judge had fulfilled his task to deliver a judgement, he was no longer obligated to the parties. Take the following text:

> D.42.1.55 (Ulpian, *Sabinus*, book 51). Once a *iudex* has given his decision (*sententia*) he ceases to be a *iudex*, and the law is that once a *iudex* has condemned someone for too much or too little, he cannot correct his decision. He has done his duty, for better or for worse, once and for all. [translation: Handouts]

The judge's decision was final and the only grounds on which it could be revisited were procedural as in the quasi-delict of the 'erring judge' which, as we have seen above, most probably referred to procedural irregularities.

Once the judgement had been delivered, the losing party had a set time in which to comply with the judgement. If he disputed the judgement, the winning party could approach the praetor once more to obtain an action on the judgement (*actio iudicati*). The losing party would then be subjected to another lawsuit based on the non-fulfilment of the original judgement. If found guilty, he would be condemned to pay twice the value of the original judgement.

> Inst.Gai.IV.9. We sue for what is ours and a penalty in those cases,

for example, in which we claim for double damages against a defendant who denies liability. This happens in the case of a judgment debt (*actio iudicati*) [translation: Handouts]

If the party did not dispute the original judgement, the winning party could proceed with the enforcement. In most cases this would involve a seizure of the belongings of the losing party to recover the value of the judgement of the court. Such a seizure of assets did not give ownership of the goods to the winning party. It merely secured the assets until such time as a curator could be appointed to oversee the selling of the goods at public auction with prior notification of other creditors so that all of the debts could be recovered.

One final point needs to be made about the decline of the formulary procedure in favour of the *cognitio*. As mentioned above, the *cognitio* was a process which evolved out of the emperor's bureaucracy. Being a product of imperial bureaucracy, it comes as little surprise that it was from this procedure that a system of appeals arose during the classical period. Under the formulary process, the decision of the judge was final and could only be revisited on the grounds of procedural irregularity. Our sources do not show the existence of any system of appeal from local or regional courts to the court of the praetor in Rome, apart from the provisions contained in the *Lex Irnitana* whereby some actions (on account of the amount of money involved or the nature of the penalty) had to be heard in Rome. Under the *cognitio*, a bureaucratic process, the idea of an appeal to a higher authority was more compatible with the nature of the process and therefore it comes as little surprise that by the end of the classical period it had become established that decisions of local courts could be appealed either to the court of the governor of a province or to the court of the praetor in Rome. The final form of appeal was directly to the emperor, who by the middle of the classical period had become an important legislator through his imperial bureaucracy.

Suggested further reading

The following books contain a more comprehensive overview of the Roman law of procedure:

Bablitz, L. *Actors and Audience in the Roman Courtroom* (Oxford 2007)
Greenidge, A. *The Legal Procedure of Cicero's Time* (Oxford 1901)
Harries, J. *Cicero and the Jurists* (London 2006)

Kelly, J.M. *Roman Litigation* (Oxford 1966)
Metzger, E. *A New Outline of the Roman Civil Trial* (Oxford 1997)
Metzger, E. *Litigation in Roman Law* (Oxford 2005)
Powell, J. and Paterson, J. (eds) *Cicero the Advocate* (Oxford 2004)

Bibliography

The narrative of this book is broadly inspired by the following works:

Buckland, W. *A Textbook on Roman Law from Augustus to Justinian*, 3rd rev. edn by P. Stein (Cambridge 1963)

Crook, J.A. *Law and Life of Rome: 90 BC-AD 212* (Ithaca, NY 1967)

Daube, D. *Roman Law: Linguistic, Social and Philosophical Aspects* (Edinburgh 1969)

Du Plessis, P.J. *Borkowski's Textbook on Roman Law*, 4th edn (Oxford 2010)

Johnston, D. *Roman Law in Context* (Cambridge 1999)

Jolowicz, H. and Nicholas, B. *A Historical Introduction to the Study of Roman Law* (Cambridge 1972)

Riggsby, A. *Roman Law and the Legal World of the Romans* (Cambridge 2010)

Robinson, O.F. *The Sources of Roman Law: Problems and Methods for Ancient Historians* (London 1997)

Schulz, F. *Classical Roman Law* (Oxford 1954)

Tellgen-Couperus, O.E. *A Short History of Roman Law* (London 1993)

The following works are cited in the text:

Berger, A. 'A labor contract of AD 164: CIL, III, P. 948, No. X', *CPh* (1948) 43: 231-42

Blume, F. *Annotated Justinian Code*, George William Hopper Law Library, http://uwacadweb.uwyo.edu/blume&justinian (last accessed 11 October 2011)

Crawford, M. (ed.) *Roman Statutes*, 2 vols (London 1996)

Gordon, W.M. and Robinson, O.F. *The Institutes of Gaius* (London 1988)

Greenidge, A. *The Legal Procedure of Cicero's Time* (Oxford 1901)

Johnston, D. *Roman Law in Context* (Cambridge 1999)

Jones, D. *The Bankers of Puteoli: Finance, Trade and Industry in the Roman World* (Stroud 2006)

Kaser, M. and Knütel, R. *Römisches Privatrecht* 17th edn (Munich 2003)

Lenel, O. *Das Edictum Perpetuum* 2nd edn (Leipzig 1907)

Riccobono, S. (ed.) *Fontes Iuris Romani Antejustiniani*, 3 vols (Florence 1940-3)

Schulz, F. *Classical Roman Law* (Oxford 1954)

Schulz, F. *The History of Roman Legal Science* (Oxford 1946)

Shelton, J. *As the Romans Did: A Sourcebook of Roman Social History*, 2nd edn (New York 1998)

Watson, A. (ed) *The Digest of Justinian*, 2 vols (rev. edn) (Philadelphia 2008)

Zimmermann, R. *The Law of Obligations: Roman Foundations of the Civilian Tradition* (Oxford 1996)

Index